The N̶...̶st Pub̶...̶

Compiled by

Caroline Belfield Clifford

Power Publications

First published in 1995 by
Power Publications
1 Clayford Avenue,
Ferndown
Dorset BH22 9PQ

ACKNOWLEDGEMENTS
I would like to thank all those in the trade who have given their time to help compile this guide. I would also like to thank Nick Hunt at the Southampton Enterprise Agency, Bill Couthard at Barclays Bank, and last but not least, my mother, for her enthusiasm and good company on the round.

Caroline B. Clifford
Coppits Cottage, Newbridge
Nr. Cadnam, Southampton

ISBN 1 898073 05 8

Edited by Mike Power
Photographs by Mike Power and Caroline Belfield Clifford
Printed by Pardy & Son (Printers) Ltd., Ringwood, Hampshire

Publisher's Note
Whilst every care has been taken to ensure that all the information in this book is accurate, neither the publishers nor the printers can accept responsibility for any inaccuracies.

Other local interest books
"Pub Walks in Hampshire"
"A Mountain Bike Guide to the Highways and Bridleways of Hampshire & The New Forest" – Summer 1995
"Mike Power's New Forest Pub Walks" – Autumn 1995

Front cover: The Royal Oak, North Gorley

INTRODUCTION

William the Conqueror created his "New Forest" in 1079, largely for his own pleasure. Today there is so much to do and see that more than 10 million visitors come to the area each year, spending around £700,000,000, 25% of this on food and drink. Public houses have responded to this demand and many now offer a great drinking venue and a high standard of cuisine, generally at a modest price.

This guide identifies that there is a pub for every occasion. You may be a first time visitor to the Forest, you may be looking for a romantic venue for dinner, you may be stuck with a screaming bunch of kids, or you may be alone, scruffy, and too tired to change. We have a pub to suit you. You might only be armed with a credit card, you might be looking for a lively band, or your only requirement may be a high chair. We can still help you.

The guide not only offers a comprehensive treatment of all the New Forest pubs within the cattle grid boundaries but also extends to cover pubs within the Heritage area and the New Forest District Area boundary.

There are many changes within the licensing trade at the moment. Most of these are due to the recession, soaring rents and the high cost of leases. As such it is impossible to keep every pub listed strictly up to date and a few properties under refurbishment have sadly been omitted. Beers stocked will naturally change as will food prices but the listings give a good idea of the type of food and price you can expect to pay.

Awards have been made as a result of comments we have received from customers. Do try all the "Don't Miss" pubs. They are real gems. And do please let us have your comments so that we can make more awards next year.

You can contact us any time at the address opposite.

I hope you enjoy The New Forest Pub Guide as much as I have, enjoyed researching it.

Caroline Belfield Clifford

CONTENTS

Rockford Green, near Ringwood. Tel (01425) 474700

The Alice Lisle takes its name from a courageous lady who gave refuge to a couple of survivors of Monmouth's 1685 rebellion. Royalists found the fugitives in the nearby Moyles Court and poor Alice was tried for treason. Despite being found not guilty by a sympathetic jury, notorious Judge Jeffreys ordered her to be burnt. After an appeal to James II for clemency her sentence was commuted - and she was beheaded instead! Alice is buried at Ellingham churchyard which is close to Rockford Green.

The Alice Lisle is a family run, Forest pub with a reputation for good food and generous helpings. There are two main bars and a restaurant-cum-family area. The cosy bar areas have been recently refurbished and have beamed ceilings and open fireplaces.

A Gales house, run by Bernard and Angela Mettale, the following beers, lagers and ciders are available on draught; Gales HSB, Alice Lisle Bitter, Gales Southdown Bitter, Wyvern LA Bitter, George Gale Dark Mild XXX (blessed three times), Guinness, Carling Black Label, Stella Artois, Fosters, Dry Blackthorn and Autumn Gold cider. There is a good selection of country wines.

The medium priced menu includes most of the pub food favourites, vegetarian dishes and a children's corner. We ordered what turned out to be a massive rack of BBQ ribs from the specials board for £5.95. When we had eaten barely half, the waitress was pleased to offer a doggy bag and explained that they were always happy to entertain any special requests and we could have asked to share the dish.

The Alice Lisle is open from 11.00 - 23.00 from Easter through to the end of September (except Sundays) and 11.00 - 15.00 and 17.00 - 23.00 in the winter season. There are 'barbies' in the summer and dinner dances out of the summer season. There is a large garden and a pet area and there is ample parking.

Angel Inn, 108 High Street, Lymington. Tel (01590) 672050

Situated across the courtyard from the Angel Inn, a 13th century coaching Inn, the Tap Room is a club bar managed by Mike Mcgoldrick and acts as the public bar for the hotel. Recently refurbished there is a large games room, bar area and comfortably decorated snug room. Games include pin ball, Pink Panther fruit machine, table football, pool, darts and juke box.

An Eldridge Pope pub, real ales on offer are Dorchester Bitter, Royal Oak and Hardy Country Bitter. Mild, Guinness, Kronenbourg, Labatts and Dry Blackthorn are also on draught.

Food is ordered from Hardy's Kitchen in the main Hotel. A traditional menu features appetisers like smoked haddock in cheese sauce £3.60, deep fried potato skins with cheese and bacon sauce £2.85 and crudities to share for £3.60. Sandwiches are priced from £1.65, steak and ale pie £4.35, jacket potatoes from £2.85, a traditional four egg omelette £3.95, chicken korma £6.45, egg and bacon brunch £2.70, sirloin steak 8oz £7.95, Hardy's grill £8.25, fish 'n' chips £3.95, cottage pie £4.35 and fried scampi £4.60. There is not much choice for vegetarians except ploughman's £3.55 or broccoli and Stilton quiche platter £3.95. Traditional Sunday roast £4.95. Daily sweet selection on the blackboard.

Bands play every Saturday and there is a disco some Fridays. Children and dogs are permitted. The Tap Room is open 11.30 - 14.30 Friday, 11.00 - 15.00 Saturday and 19.00 - 23.00 every day. Sunday opening 12.00 - 14.30. Note that the Hotel bar has also been refurbished and is open from 10.00. The Inn is supposed to be haunted both by a little girl who sits on the stairs and by a cavalier presumed killed in the bar. Reasonably priced en-suite accommodation with TV, tea and coffee making facilities and full English breakfast: single from £29.50, double £47.50 and four poster suites £65.

Lyndhurst Road, Cadnam. Tel (01703) 283677

Built in 1759 as a hunting lodge, this secluded hotel is a Forest treasure with its superb interior with oak panelled entrance hall, minstrel's gallery and fireplace. In the hotel brochure it is described as a civilised retreat - I would definitely agree. Hunters bar is ideal for a lunchtime snack or pre-dinner drinks and non-residents are welcome. The cosy bar also serves as a popular venue for car clubs.

Ringwood Best Bitter is the real ale with Tetley Bitter and Carlsberg also on draught.

Simple bar snacks include toasted double decker sandwiches such as bacon, lettuce and tomato from £3.95, cheese salad sandwich £2.50, prawn and mayonnaise sandwich £3.95 and smoked salmon sandwich £4.50. Watch the blackboard for special offers including set meals in the imposing restaurant.

The bar is open all day. Credit cards welcome. Attractive grounds. Tudor Room for private functions.

THE BAT AND BALL INN 4

Breamore, near Fordingbridge. Tel (01725) 22252

The Bat and Ball was converted into a hostelry from a common ale house in the last century when the "Southampton" (presumably Hampshire) cricket team came to play in the area. It is a genuine local's country pub, popular with the villagers and also visiting fishermen as the owners Joe and Phyllis White have nearby fishing rights. The pub undoubtedly has a lot of history surrounding it and a ghostly nun, possibly a visitor from a nearby priory demolished in Henry VIII's time. Just up the road is Breamore House where the curse of the Dodington's is said to fall upon anyone who touches a certain painting. Recently a villager dusting the painting died the same afternoon by falling off his roof at home while fixing a TV aerial!

The pub boasts a spacious through bar with real fires and an unobtrusive restaurant. This free house offers a frequently changing selection of ales such as Bass, Bass Special, Ruddles Best Bitter, 12 Bore Traditional, Ringwood Best Bitter and Wadworth 6X, Autumn Gold cider is also on draught.

The extensive bar menu features whitebait garni and prawn cocktail both £2.50, grilled trout £4.50, chicken pasta bake, chips and salad, and leek, cheese and potato bake both £3.75. Snacks range from sandwiches from £1.75 to filled jacket potatoes from £2.00. Sweets from £1.75. Restaurant fayre includes king prawns in garlic butter £5 fillet of plaice £5.25, 14oz. Children's menu.

Opening hours are 11.00 - 15.00 and 17.30 - 23.00 Monday to Saturday and the normal Sunday hours. There is a dart board, occasional live music and a large garden. Well behaved dogs on leads allowed. Accommodation is offered at £20 for a single room and £32 double. Most major credit cards are accepted.

BEAULIEU ROAD PUB 5

Beaulieu Road, Lyndhurst. Tel (01703) 292342

Situated in an isolated position on Beaulieu Heath, halfway between Beaulieu and Lyndhurst at Beaulieu Road Station, this friendly pub has a view of the forest and the pony sales yard. Originally the adjoining hotel stables, the pub has been tastefully refurbished and designed with the bar area being neatly separated from the long, narrow and popular restaurant. Flagstone floors, wattle ceiling, and warming open fires create a welcoming atmosphere which is enhanced by the unusual hat collection that festoons the ceiling.

The pub is owned by Care Hotels and managed by Ian Newman. Courage Directors, Wadworth 6X and a guest real ale are tapped straight from the cask. Also on draught are John Smiths Bitter, Courage Dark Mild, Guinness, Carlsberg, Holsten Export and Dry Blackthorn cider.

The wide-ranging and good value menu includes Forest broth and crusty bread £1.45, calamares £2.20, country pâté £2.25, followed by double sausage with chips or jacket potato £2.70, sirloin steak in french bread £3.25, turkey and leek pie £4.70, beef and ale pie £4.50, pork in cider apple sauce £4.75, brunch grill with bacon, sausage, beefburger, tomato, mushrooms and egg £4.95. Children's menu.

There is an extensive landscaped garden with children's play area. Sunday evening is 60's night. Children are allowed in the restaurant area. No dogs. Opening hours are 11.00 - 15.00 and 18.00 - 23.00 Monday to Friday in the winter but all day in the summer. All day Saturday and normal Sunday hours. The hotel has 18 en-suite rooms all with colour TV and tea and coffee making facilities. Bed and breakfast from £44 single and from £68 double.

THE BELL INN   6

Brook, near Cadnam. Tel (01703) 812214   * "Good Food" award

Although the Bell Inn has recently been refurbished to bring it up to three-star standard, it is far from being just another hotel bar. It is the meeting place for local farmers, businessmen and dignitaries alike and offers something for everyone. The food is excellent, the atmosphere friendly and the staff polite - the sort that remember you from your previous visit. The original building dates back to 1782 and many period features are still in evidence. The uncluttered bar has an old inglenook fireplace, and antique prints of rural scenes recall the history of the Bell as a drover's halt and hunting lodge. The Bell has been owned by the Scott family throughout its history, and behind the hotel and under the same control is the Bramshaw Golf Club with its two 18-hole courses.

A free house, it offers a varying selection of real ales, such as Ringwood Best Bitter, Wadworth 6X and Draught Bass, Worthington Best Bitter, Tetley Bitter, Guinness, Tennent's Pilsner and Extra, and Dry Blackthorn cider.

Featured in some of the top guides, the Bell is noted for its range of high standard and value-for-money meals. Snacks include sandwiches £2.50 and favourites like Drover's lunch and New Forest pasties. Specialising in local game and fresh fish from Poole, the imaginative specials board is the menu to choose from and on the day of visiting included tartare of smoked fish with cucumber dressing £3.75, sauté chicken livers with cream and brandy £3.65, moules mariniére £2.75, American sea bass, peppers and lemon £6.25, fillet of salmon, herb mousseline £6.25 with chocolate torte and compote of oranges £2.75 for dessert. Family room with highchairs and children's menu and cutlery.

The Bell is open all day in summer with cream teas in the afternoon. Winter times are 11.00 - 15.00 and 18.00 - 23.00. Normal Sunday opening. All credit cards accepted. Accommodation prices according to season.

BOLD FORESTER   7

Beaulieu Road, Marchwood. Tel (01703) 865967

Managed by Guy and Claire Mayger, this is a Country Carvery property with a good family atmosphere midday and a younger crowd in the evenings. The main bar is spacious with brick, beams, taped music and crystal maze. The restaurant is equally large and there is a family room, skittle alley, pool, darts and petanque. Outside there are lots of children's activities including a bouncy castle.

This is a Courage house with Websters Bitter, John Smith's Bitter and Ruddles County. Also on draught are Holsten Export, Fosters, Calsberg, Mild, Watney's, Websters Yorkshire Bitter, Guinness, Scrumpy Jack and Stongbow cider.

Bar snacks are available but the Bold Forester specialises in their three course meal £9.49. To start with there is soup of the day or a very appetising choice of cold starters from the 'starters bar'. The carvery includes at least three roast joints such as prime rib, roast turkey and lamb. Vegetables and traditional trimmings are included. Desserts include a range of gateaux, fruits and ice creams. Vegetarian main couses include curry, avocado and corn bake or tagliatelle Alfredo. Two courses cost £6.49 and one course carvery £4.49. All the food is fresh and appetising - 'back to basics!' House wine £6.99 per bottle. There is a children's menu but kids eat free Sunday 14.30 to 17.30.

All credit cards are accepted except Switch and Diners. Dogs are allowed. High chairs available. The Bold Forester is open all day, 11.00 - 23.00 Monday to Saturday during the summer but afternoon closing during the winter.

BOLTON'S BENCH INN   8

Southampton Road, Lyndhurst. Tel (01703) 282262   * "Management" award

This attractive cottage is more than just a pub, for it aims to cater for everyone, offering good accommodation, party facilities, and afternoon cream teas. Visitors will find a warm welcome and it is justifiably popular with both tourists, locals and walkers. The building has been a tea house - before being bought by the enterprising Rosaleen Weeks in 1991. There is one long bar and comfortable seating in cosy rooms with squashy sofas, and a separate restaurant area.

As a free house a good selection of well kept ales are available, namely Ringwood Best Bitter, Draught Bass and a regularly changing guest beer such as Castle Eden Ale. Also served on draught are Worthington Best Bitter, Murphys, Mild, Tennent's Extra, Carling Black Label, Heineken and Strongbow cider.

The bar menu features homemade soup £1.50, whitebait £3.25, beefburger £3.25, lasagne £4.75, cottage pie £4.25 and vegetarian dishes from £4.25. Lighter bites include ploughman's from £3.25 and sandwiches from £1.50. The restaurant menu specialises in home prepared food such as the freshly prepared garlic mushrooms. Dishes include lamb and vegetable broth (a meal on its own) £2.00, steak, kidney and Guinness pie £5.00, chicken and garlic en croute £8.50, Scotch sirloin £9.25 and a three course roast dinner from £8.00. Children's meal £6.00.

Further facilities include disabled toilets, bucket seats for the elderly and two gardens, one prohibiting children and dogs.

Opening hours are from 11.00 - 23.00 except Monday when it opens 18.00 - 23.00. Normal licensing hours Sunday but food is served all day. Three en-suite rooms with colour TV from £37.50 according to season.

THE BOSUN'S CHAIR   9

Station Street, Lymington. Tel (01590) 675140

Originally called the Railway Inn, the building dates back to the opening of the railway on July 12th 1858 and is part of the extensive smugglers tunnel network that criss-crosses Lymington. The spacious interior has a nautical theme.

Landlords, Stuart Hopkinson and Jo Gibbard run this Wadworth pub and serve three real ales - Bass, Wadworth 6X and IPA - on handpump. Also on draught are John Smiths Bitter, Guinness, Red Stripe, Heineken, Stella Artois and Dry Blackthorn cider.

Medium priced bar snacks start at £3.95 for a large pizza with salad, chemula turkey pitta or fresh grilled mackerel and extend to a range of unusual spicy dishes. Also on the menu are jacket potatoes filled with prawns £2.95, ham, chicken and mushroom pie £3.95, steak and kidney pie £3.95 and battered cod £3.95. More imaginative fayre can be ordered in the restaurant which specialises in fresh fish; starters include blazing red fish fillets £2.50, langoustine soup £2.25 and octopus salad £2.95. Main courses range from langoustine and tuna steak with cream and spinach sauce £8.95 to king scallops in bacon, cream and sherry sauce £8.95 and sauté duck breast with raspberry and cranberry sauce for £10.45. New Forest ice creams £2.25 to finish. English breakfast £3 from 9.30 in the summer.

Dogs and children are most welcome inside and on fine days children will be kept amused at the pets corner in the garden. Credit cards are accepted. Opening hours are from 11.00 - 23.00 Monday to Saturday with normal Sunday hours. 'Happy hours' are from 17.00 to 19.00 Friday when there is 50p off doubles and pints. Live music every Sunday, summer barbecues and en-suite accommodation with Sky TV (£30 single, £40 double). Car park and beer garden at rear.

BRIDGE TAVERN   10

Ipers Bridge, Fawley. Tel (01703) 892554

This is still a real pub rather than an eating house. Landlord Simon Herd and his wife Paula have a sense of humour and will give you a friendly welcome when you call in. The ceiling is wood panelled, there is a piano and a number of water colours by Rachel Long on the walls. The real fire gives a cheery atmosphere in winter. The public bar with darts board is simply decorated but clean and cosy.

This is a Whitbread leasehold with Ringwood Best Bitter, Winter Royal and Fortyniner on handpump. Whitbread Best Biter, Guinness, Murphys stout, Mild, Heineken, Stella Artois, Red Rock and Strongbow cider on draught.

All food is prepared on the premises and reasonably priced. The menu is on a blackboard and may include baguettes filled with cheese, ham or egg salad for £1.60, jacket potatoes from £2.20, homemade parsnip and apple soup £1.60, Ardennes pâté £1.60, deep fried mushrooms with stilton or garlic dip £1.80, chilli con carne £3.75, homemade steak and kidney pie £4.15, chicken breast in a creamy leek sauce £6.50, omelettes with a choice of filling £3.75, beef stew with herby dumplings £3.50, Scottish salmon with a lemon butter sauce £6.50 and freshly prepared pizzas for £3.75.

There is live entertainment most Friday nights and a quiz every other Sunday night. Children are allowed, and dogs in the public bar. Caravan site and B&B close by. There is a riverside beer garden and children's play area. The Bridge Tavern is open all day 11.00 - 23.00, six days a week with normal Sunday opening.

THE CARPENTERS ARMS   11

Burley Road, Bransgore, Christchurch. Tel (01425) 672295

Dating from the turn of the century, this popular pub has been recently redecorated to give a rustic, barn-like appearance with lots of oak beams and old sturdy furnishings in cosy booths. Old carpenter's tools adorn the walls. Ostensibly a family pub managed by Richard Morely, the Carpenters has a garden with play equipment, swings, sandpit, children's room, disabled toilet and, unusually, provides "baby meals". Horse rails and water are provided for those who prefer to ride to the pub.

Owned by Eldridge Pope, the pub dispenses their Dorchester Bitter, Royal Oak, Hardy Country Ale, a guest and Blackdown Porter on handpump. Also available are EP Best Bitter, M&B Mild, Guinness, Labatt's, Faust, Swan Light Low Alcohol and Dry Blackthorn cider plus an extensive range of bottled "designer" lagers.

This is a popular eating house, the straightforward menu listing prawn cocktail £2.10, filled jacket potatoes from £2.25, salads from £3.60, trawlerman's ploughman's with smoked mackerel £2.65, basket meals from £3.85, locally caught trout £4.25 and sirloin steak £7.95. The specials board concentrates on traditional country pies - rabbit, pheasant and roast duck, £3.95 - £7.95. Sweets again are traditional if not homemade - chocolate fudge cake, lemon lush and fruits of the Forest - all £2.05.

The pub is involved with a lot of charity work and recently purchased three guide dogs. Dogs are welcome inside. Pool room, darts, crib, dominoes, juke box, five-a-side football and regular live entertainment, either music or a comedian, on Fridays or Saturdays.

Opening hours are from 11.00 - 14.30 Monday till Thursday, (Friday and Saturday till 15.00) and 18.00 - 23.00. Sunday closing at 14.30.

Whitsbury, near Fordingbridge. Tel (017253) 362   * "Real Ale" award

Tucked away off the beaten track in a peaceful village, the Cartwheel is an unusual pub with an attractive "cottage" frontage, a low-beamed main bar with horse racing decorations, a snug games bar and a small intimate dining room. Originaly a barn back in the 1880's, then a bakery and a wheelwright's, hence its name, it is now the focal point of the tranquil village of Whitsbury which is famous for its successful racing stables and for being the home of Britain's most famous racehorse, Desert Orchid (Dessie) before his retirement. A mixed clientele includes local stable lads and visitors from further afield seeking out the varied selection of real ales and good food.

This popular free house dispenses six regularly changing real ales and last year no less than 120 brews were pulled through the handpumps. Guest ales include such exciting names as Adnams Broadside, Theakstons Old Peculiar, Greene King Abbot Ale, Ringwood Fortyniner, Banks and Taylor Dragonslayer, Morland Old Speckled Hen, Goldfinch, Flashmans Clout Ale and Bunces Vice Beer. There are six lagers on draught and for cider drinkers, Copperhead, Addlestone's, Old English and Gaymer's.

The Cartwheel is also distinguished as having one of the longest menus in the area. Light snacks include sandwiches from £1, smoked mackerel ploughman's £2.90 served with granary bread, salad garnish and pickles. Other dishes featured are seafood au gratin £3.60, shell-on Norwegian prawns £2.15, steak and kidney pudding £4.70, 8oz peppered rump steak "Cartwheel style" £8.20, wholemeal smoked salmon quiche £3.90, and creamy mushroom parmagiana £3.85.

Opening hours are from 11.00 - 14.30 and 18.00 - 23.00 Monday to Saturday, and the usual Sunday hours. Meals are available all week except Tuesday evening. There is an attractive sloping garden with an exciting shute for children. Dogs are welcome in the garden and bar if on a lead.

Hinton Admiral, near Christchurch. Tel (01425) 276050

If you thought this was just another Harvester eating house then you would be missing a busy pub, and the meeting place for the local community from the nearby villages. The high volume, main restaurant is neat and crisp but the long, yet cosy, bar with its bench seats, open fire, low, beamed ceilings and stone tiled floor attracts personalities from far afield, and has done so for many years. In the 11th century, as recorded in the Domesday Book, a hospice - "house of St. Catherine the Faithful" - on this same site, was run by monks of Christchurch Priory to offer shelter to New Forest travellers. Later, in the 18th century this was a popular haunt of smugglers operating in Christchurch bay, their contraband being hidden in the chimneys. Manager, licensee and self-acclaimed ring master, Graham Warren, claims that there is something for everyone in this attractive, thatched, 300-year-old pub.

The Cat and Fiddle is a free house with a menu of some 15 real ales, normally a selection of three at any time - Draught Bass, Courage Directors and Ruddles County Bitter on handpump. Also on draught are John Smiths Bitter, Beamish, Fosters, Kronenbourg and Dry Blackthorn cider.

If you choose from the Harvester menu, two courses will cost you between £7-10 and includes an exciting salad bar. The pub menu includes harvest country soup £2.55, prawn'n crab jacket potato £1.99, hickory smoked ribs £3.55, battered prawns £3.75 and bakehouse plaits from £3.25. For those with a sweet tooth, try "Rocky Horror", a monstrous bowl of hot chocolate fudge cake shrouded with chocolate ice cream and veiled with chocolate sauce £2.45.

There is a large garden with kids equipment. The restaurant seats 120 and has a no-smoking area. Highchairs for kids and disabled toilets. All major credit cards except Diners. Guide dogs only. The Cat and Fiddle is open all day, 11.00 - 23.00, every day, May to September. In the winter season 11.00 - 15.00 and 17.00 - 23.00.

45, St. Thomas Street, Lymington. Tel (01590) 672004

Situated at the top of the High Street, almost opposite Waitrose, Champagne Charlie's is the "seafood king" of Lymington, serving restaurant food at pub prices. The building dates from around 1700, has a ghost, and has been used as both a mortuary and a brothel.

The bar is decorated in a marine theme with sea paintings, prints and nets. The atmosphere is one of unpretentious fun, largely due to the non-stop humour of the landlord, Charlie, who claims that the bar is open all day, or until he falls over.

The pub is owned by Eldridge Pope and serves real ales Royal Oak, Hardy Country Ale and Dorchester Bitter. Guinness, Blackthorn Cidermaster, Carlsberg and Faust are on draught, and of course, Champagne by the glass.

The speciality is seafood but the menu does include all the old pub favourites. Appetizers include spicy chicken buffalo wings £3.95, crab thermidor £5.95, bowl of shell-on prawns £3.25, rollmop herrings hors d'ouevres £2.50 and whitebait £3.50. Entrée's include today's local catch which could be plaice, Dover sole, skate or mussels, and come in small medium and large portions from £4.25, fisherman's pie £4.25, moussaka £4.25 or steak and kidney pie £4.25. There are ploughman's lunches at £2.95, salads from £4.25 and basket meals from £3.95.

There are no distractions in the form of juke box, pool or live music. Both children and dogs are welcome.

The bar is open all day from 10.00 - 23.00. Food is also served till 10.30 on Saturday or depending on demand. Give a call if you are in doubt.

THE CHEQUERS INN 15

Ridgeway Lane, Lower Woodside, Lymington. Tel (01590) 673415

* "Don't Miss" award

Chequers is an attractive, unspoilt pub with rough cast walls and wood and stone floors. There are water colours by Sally Hamilton for sale, an open fire, beams, pub mirrors, old photographs of Lymington and a rustic atmosphere with yachting connections. The clientele is cliquy but the pub is fun. Run by Mike and Maggie Jamieson this "off the beaten track" treasure should not be missed.

At the time of visiting Chequers real ales were Flowers Original, Wadworth 6X, Draught Bass and Cornish Original Bitter. Whitbread Best, Guinness, Heineken, Stella Artois, Stonehouse and Dry Blackthorn cider are also on draught.

The pub is renowned for its excellent food and restaurant style menu. The 'slightly separate' restaurant area is petite and very pretty with festoon blinds and lots of greenery. The menu is written on the blackboard and includes such favourites as moules mariniere £3.25, sauté ducks liver on a bed of salad £3.95, homemade beef broth £2.00, hot garlic prawns £3.75, melted Camembert and tomatoes £3.75, avocado and seafood salad £3.75, cod au gratin £6.50, lemon sole £7.95, fillet of brill with lime butter £8.95, chicken Egyptian £7.25, tenderloin of pork with mustard sauce £7.50, Chequers mixed grill £8.50, half roast Aylesbury duck £9.25 and roast rack of lamb with redcurrant and mint £7.95. Desserts are exotic and priced at £2.25. In the winter, a selection of exotic sausages such as beef and garlic are served with mashed potato and mushy peas for around £4.00.

Dogs and children are permitted although this is recommended as an adult pub. There is a sheltered garden and pretty patio area.

Chequers is open from 11.00 - 14.30ish and 18.00 - 23.00 Monday to Saturday, and normal Sunday hours. Mastercard and Visa.

Daggons Road, Alderholt, near Fordingbridge. Tel (01425) 652147

The Churchill Arms is a large 19th century village pub with one main bar decorated in a modern style and featuring most amenities. Licensee, Paul Henshaw, has managed the pub for 17 years and has an equally loyal and friendly staff.

The pub is owned by Hall and Woodhouse and there is an interesting selection of beers and lagers available on draught, including their Badger Best Bitter and Charles Wells Eagle Bitter. Murphys, Munchener Pilsner Lager, Hofbrau Export, Royal Hofbrau and Taunton Cider are also served on draught.

There is a typical pub menu and a daily specials board. Main menu dishes include ploughman's £2.50, haddock £3.95, scampi £4.75, homemade steak and kidney pie £4.75, rump steak £8.25, gammon and pineapple £5.25 and whole lemon sole stuffed with crab £5.35. The specials board may list lasagne £4.25 and salads, for example fresh salmon £6.75. Busy weekend and holiday fayre features fresh fish such as cod, haddock, dressed crab, halibut steaks, mussels or a full one and a quarter pound plaice or lemon sole £4.75 to £7.50. Sweets are upmarket, trendy creations, namely heaven on earth, honour cassis, blackboard chequers and various gâteaux from £1.95. Children's dishes from £1.95.

Opening hours are from 11.00 - 15.00 and 18.00 - 23.00 Monday to Saturday and normal Sunday hours. There is a functions room, a skittle alley, a bandit machine, videos and garden with swings. High chairs are available for young children and well behaved dogs welcome inside.

THE COACH AND HORSES 17

Southampton Road, Cadnam. Tel (01703) 813120

The Coach and Horses is a local pub with time for the passer-by. The board outside claims that it is the last real pub for 24,000 miles East or West - I'll leave you to work that one out for yourself. There is a main bar in need of some redecoration, and behind the pub, a hall where a number of the popular "music nights" are held. There are padded bench seats, old photographs of Cadnam, a piano, net curtains and a gas fire. If you just want to relax, be yourself and take in the lack of local culture you will enjoy the Coach.

A Whitbread pub, the Coach and Horses serves real ales, namely Flowers Original, Ringwood Best Bitter and Wadworth 6X. Whitbread Best Bitter, Mild, Guinness, Heineken, Stella Artois and Strongbow cider are also on draught. Richard Chamberlain look-alike landlord, John Symes, prides himself on keeping the cost of a good pint down and prices are amongst the cheapest in the area. Do check out the photograph behind the bar of John and his wife Ursula if you doubt the reference above. They have been at the helm 18 years, almost a record!

Shop price bar snacks are available but in the winter months food is restricted to cheese, ham, beef, chicken and tomato sandwiches or rolls, mostly at £1.10.

Pub games and live entertainment are the pub priorities, darts and dominoes are played regularly, jazz is featured every Friday, bingo on the first Tuesday of the month and a piano sing-a-long with Roger on Sunday evenings. The pub boasts a welcoming atmosphere for all age groups.

The Coach and Horses opens 12 noon to 15.00 and 18.00 - 23.00 and the normal Sunday hours. Unfenced garden with bench seating and both dogs and children are allowed inside. Coaches welcome.

THE COMPASSES INN 18

Damerham, near Fordingbridge. Tel (017253) 231

This is an attractive country inn with its own oast house, in the pretty hamlet of Damerham. The public bar is lively but cosy with two open fires, while the spick and span lounge is tastefully decorated with floral wallpaper and curtains, has a log fire and a separate dining area. Dating back 400 years, the pub is famous as being the place where Captain Cook was captured and has a car park that is supposedly haunted by a ghostly stage-coach.

This is a Whitbread pub serving regular real ales - Flowers Original, Wadworth 6X, Ringwood Best Bitter - and a guest ale such as Balkesbury New Ale. Murphys stout, Heineken, Stella Artois and Dry Blackthorn cider are also on draught.

Landlord, James Kidd, has introduced an extensive menu with around twelve specials listed on a blackboard. Dishes include devilled whitebait £3.00, tagliatelli with tuna and cream sauce £3.25, steak and mushroom pie £5.25, rump steak £7.95, sauté chicken with sherry, cream and mushroom sauce £7.25 and local trout pan-fried with parsley £7.25. Specials may feature duck with juniper and rosemary sauce £7.95 and bass with mushrooms and Madeira £8.95. For dessert try the range of ice-creams £1.95 or spotted dick £2.25. Also available are vegetarian dishes and children's meals from £1.95. The food is good and cooked to order.

The Compasses Inn is open 11.00 - 14.30 and 18.00 - 23.00, all day Saturday and normal Sunday hours. Visa, Mastercard and Access accepted. Children are welcome away from the bar and dogs are allowed in the public bar. Garden with play area and en-suite overnight accommodation (£24.50 single, £43 double). Campsite and fish farm nearby.

Winsor Road, Winsor, near Cadnam. Tel (01703) 812237   * "Don't Miss" award

Tucked away in the tiny village of Winsor, just outside the Forest boundary, the Compass Inn is one of the most welcoming pubs we visited. The pub is an unspoilt, unpretentious, country pub estimated to be about 300 hundred-years-old, with low beams, a real fire and a cosy atmosphere. Being off the main routes it mainly attracts a local crowd and you will find yourself rubbing shoulders with foresters of varied trades some legitimate, some not so!

The Compass is a Whitbread partnership ably run by Ian and Sandra McKenna. Real ales are well kept and include Flowers Original, Boddingtons Bitter, Ringwood Best, Fuller's London Pride, Gales HSB, Wadworth 6X and Strong Country Bitter. Whitbread Best Bitter, Heineken, Stella Artois, Guinness, Murphys stout, Inches and Strongbow cider are also on draught.

Food is good, reasonably priced and homemade. Sandra makes her own bread and serves an excellent open sandwich and there is also an 'all day breakfast' £3.75, filled jacket potato from £2.25, wholetail scampi in golden crumbs £3.95, beef stew and bread £2.50, hickory smoked ribs £5.50 (you can share these), broccoli and cauliflower cheese £3.75, sausage, chips and beans £2.50, lasagne verdi £3.75 and other pub favourites. The puddings change daily but there is always freshly baked carrot cake 90p a slice, trifles, fruit pies and ice cream, all £1.50 and served as you would like it. We also found the pub very accommodating as far as the time that food is served, although note that the kitchen is closed on Tuesday.

Opening hours are 11.00 - 15.00 (flexible) and 18.00 - 23.00 and normal Sunday hours. TV in the public bar, fruit machine, pool and darts. Background music. Dogs welcome in the public bar, children in the family area and there is a garden with swings. And yes, there is a ghost, an old lady who drinks gin!

THE CROWN HOTEL   20

Lyndhurst. Tel (01703) 282922

Situated at the top of the High Street, opposite the church where Alice Liddell (of Alice in Wonderland fame) is buried, the site was probably used as stables for Charles I and lodgings for his retinue and many hangers on. The original building was built in 1600 and rebuilt as a coaching inn in 1897. The staff will be happy to show you a book with a full history of the Crown. The cosy panelled bar has elegant stone arches, leather chairs and stag heads.

Real ales on handpump are Courage Best, Courage Directors and Ringwood Best Bitter.

The bar menu includes starters of avocado and feta cheese salad £2.50 and local smoked seafood £3.95. Main courses include steak, mushroom and Guinness pie £4.95, Scottish sirloin steak £8.95, lemon chicken breast £5, poached fresh salmon £6.50, venison sausages £4.95, warm chicken livers with mixed lettuce £3.25, and for the vegetarian, spinach, tomato and egg fusilli £3.95 and deep-fried avocado and mushrooms £4.00. There is a specials board and a children's menu.

The bar is open 11.00 - 14.30 and 18.30 - 23.00 six days a week with normal Sunday hours. There is a quiet garden and car park at the rear.

THE CROWN INN   21

Southampton Street, Ringwood. Tel (01425) 472708

Originally a 17th century coaching Inn, town jail and magistrates court, the Crown comprises the cosy Fish and Crown bars, a restaurant, function room and the Crown Tap for a younger crowd. Largely unmodernised with a tiled floor, the traditional Fish and Crown bars could hardly be called typical of Eldridge Pope properties. Exposed beams, plates, copper nick-nacks, old photographs and cased fish break up the blood red ceiling and nicotine yellow walls. The fish collection is well renowned and people come from miles around to inspect the spectacular specimens, all caught locally. If you hate getting change for, and fighting with, cigarette machines offering part empty packs of over-priced cigarettes, then this is one of the few pubs in the Forest to still sell cigarettes from behind the bar.

The Crown dispenses EP Best Bitter, Guinness, Carlsberg, Carlsberg Export, Labatt's and Dry Blackthorn cider on draught and the brewery's real ales include Dorchester Bitter and Hardy Country Ale on handpump.

Typical pub fayre appears on the lunchtime and bar snack menu. Appetizers include prawn cocktail £2.75 and crispy mushrooms £2.60, followed by a mini-mixed grill with lamb cutlet, gammon, kidney, sausage, mushroom and tomato £4.25 and chicken Kiev £4.50. There is a vegetarian choice, dinner jackets, plough person's, super sarnies and meals for minor diners. The specials board may feature roast pork and apple sauce £3.95 and Normandy pork with vegetables £2.75. Sweets £1.99 and range from spotted dick, treacle sponge, and hot chocolate sponge, to cherry pie and death by chocolate.

Dogs and children most welcome inside. Visa and Access accepted. There is a juke box and darts in the Tap Bar and seven bedrooms are available for bed and breakfast £16 per person.

The bars are open for a long day, from 10.00 - 23.00 from Monday to Saturday, and normal Sunday hours.

CROWN INN 22

High Street, Fordingbridge. Tel (01425) 652552

This former coaching inn is an unspoilt, character filled, green and cream painted town pub which dates back to the 1600's and one can still see the original stables with mangers. Over the fireplace is a picture of old Fordingbridge in the days when you could see from the High Street right down to the river. There is very little clutter and although there is just one bar it gives the impression of being several rooms with a cosy fireplace, barrel seats and settles.

A Whitbread pub inn run for the last 14 years by landlords Chris and Marion Bell. Real ales featured here are Flowers Original, Fullers London Pride, Strong Country Bitter and two guest ales, such as Old Speckled Hen and Batemans XXXB. Whitbread Best, Guinness, Murphys stout, Heineken, Stella Artois, Dry Blackthorn and Burrow Hill Farmhouse cider are also on draught.

There is a small, separate dining area and a bar menu which offers sandwiches from £1.50, ploughman's from £3.25, traditional Dorset pâté £3.75, hot chilli Mexican with garlic bread £4.95, steak and Guinness pie £5.25, beef curry with pompadom £5.25, and an 8-9oz fillet steak £11.50. Chris makes his own pizzas, from £3.95, in a special oven and they can be either eaten on the premises or taken away. Sweet selection £1.95. There is a Saturday night specials menu including grilled Avon trout with a lemon, white wine, herb and butter sauce £7.25, Scotch salmon steak á la meuniéré £9.50 and duck a l'orange £11.50.

The Crown is open from 11.00 - 15.00 and 17.00 - 23.00 weekdays, all day Saturday depending on business, normal Sunday hours. Coach parties can be catered for. En-suite overnight accommodation with all facilities at £35 per double.

CROWN INN 23

Old Christchurch Road, Everton, Lymington. Tel (01590) 642655

The Crown Inn is a traditional village pub tucked off the main Lymington to Christchurch Road at Everton and has a history dating back some 500 years when it was originally known as the Yeovilton Post House. The village was once called Yeovilton, or "evil town", a name associating the village with witchcraft and a story that horses eating the foliage, died. According to Kelly's Directory the first landlord appeared in the Crown in the 1870's. Licensee, Paul Lines, an ex RN Submariner, is not slow to blow his own trumpet, clearly demonstrating his charismatic and entertaining character. The trade is mainly local but any visitors will be made welcome and will find the pub very friendly. There is a comfortable lounge bar with real fire and beams and a separate, cosy public bar.

The Crown is a Whitbread pub serving their Flowers Original, Strong Country Bitter, as well as Draught Bass and a guest ale. Whitbread Best, Guinness, Heineken, Stella Artois and Strongbow cider are also on draught.

The food is good and reasonably priced and available every session with the exception of Sunday night. Sandwiches from £1.25, soup £1.50, ploughman's from £3.25, basket meals from £3.50, macaroni cheese £4.00, gammon steak £6.50, steak and all the trimmings £7.50 and a daily specials board. These dishes include lasagne £4.50, chilli with jacket potato or rice £4.50 and ham, egg and chips £3.75. Sweets include syrup sponge pudding and custard £1.75, and banana split £2.00.

There is a garden with swings and barbecue area. Dogs are allowed in the public bar and garden if kept under strict control. Children welcome. Outside seating and hit and miss street parking. Opening hours are from 11.00 - 14.30 and 18.00 - 23.00 Monday to Saturday and normal Sunday hours.

Ringwood Road, Bransgore, near Christchurch. Tel (01425) 672279

Located in the centre of Bransgore, the first building in the village, the 200-year-old Crown Inn is a smaller, more personal version of the typical Brewers Fayre property. This friendly pub, run by Michael and Lynette Hazelton, is a popular lunchtime eating place, with a younger crowd filling the bar in the evenings. There is one bar which has been recently refurbished and has a good dining area and a snug corner atttractively decorated in Laura Ashley-style.

The standard Whitbread products are available plus a selection of real ales served by handpump, namely, Flowers Original, Wadworth 6X and Marstons Pedigree. Also available on draught are Whitbread Best Bitter, Heineken, Stella Artois, Strongbow cider and a well kept selection of wines.

The menu is Brewers Fayre and offers inexpensive, good value dishes. Starters include fish dippers - selected pieces of fish and prawn deep fried and served with a dip £2.50, farmhouse pâté £1.75, smoked trout fillet £1.95 and crispy vegetable and chicken parcels £1.75, followed by steak and kidney pie £3.65, chicken escalopes with lemon £4.85, fillet of salmon £5.45, Stilton and broccoli quiche £3.55 and lasagne with crusty bread or French fries £4.35. Salads, sandwiches and light bites from £1.60 and traditional roast Sunday lunch £4.75 are also served. Food is available all day 11.30 to 22.00 from 12 noon Sunday. House wine from £4.95.

The bar is open all day, every day. Families are well catered for; outside there is a well equipped garden play area and pets corner, while inside there are baby 'nappy' changing facilities and highchairs for younger diners. Bar billiards and traditional pub games. Access and Visa accepted.

Clayhill, Lyndhurst. Tel (01703) 282272

Situated south of Lyndhurst on one of the main tourist routes through the Forest, the Crown and Stirrup enjoys a mix of visitors and a local clientele. The building dates back to the 13th century and is listed in Beaulieu Abbey. The name of the pub should probably be the "Crown Stirrup", the reason being that this is the building where the "Royal stirrup" was kept. If you were a peasant during Tudor times and you wanted to keep a dog, it was necessary that the dog was small enough to pass through the stirrup, otherwise it was considered a threat to the royal hunting, and would at the very least, have its claws removed. The stirrup is now kept at Queen's House at the Verderer's Court in Lyndhurst.

The pub has a very attractive exterior and cosy interior refurbished by licensees Mark and Kim Pycroft. The comfortable main bar has a real fire, low ceilings with exposed wooden beams, painted wood panels and a small rear snug.

A Whitbread partnership serving Castle Eden Ale, Boddingtons Bitter and Fullers London Pride real ales with Whitbread Best Bitter, Mild, Heineken, Stella Artois and Scrumpy Jack cider also on draught.

Mark is in charge of the kitchen and offers an exciting, medium priced menu which includes pan fried sardines in garlic butter £4.25, baked avocado with wild mushroom sauce, and labskaus both £4.25, potato and onion pancakes served with apple sauce £2.75, rack of lamb served with raspberry vinegar sauce £8.25 and fillet steak £10.25. There is a daily changing specials and a sweets board; all sweets £2.25. Children's meals. Regular theme evenings are proving very popular.

The bar is open 11.00 - 15.00 and 17.30 - 23.00 weekdays and normal Sunday hours. There is a garden at the rear with a children's play area.

Hamptworth, near Landford, Wiltshire. Tel (01794) 390302 * "Don't Miss" award
* "Real Ale" award

If you take the A36, Southampton to Salisbury road, and turn off at the Landford Poacher on the B3079 you will find this "off the beaten track", unspoilt gem of a country pub, owned by Jean and Derrick Proudley.

The Cuckoo is a 300 year old, thatched, listed building, part of which was once the village shop that used to dispense draught cider whilst preparing the orders. It has been a pub since the 1930's and comprises a tiny bar and four small and cosy rooms, two of them suitable for children. Decidedly rustic in both furnishings and decor with an assortment of tables and chairs, bird pictures and a warming open fire.

A family pub and popular free house, it draws lovers of real ale into its homely confines to sample traditional ales drawn straight from the cask and served in the traditional way in prime condition. At the time we visited the pub there were twelve real ales on offer, with a different guest beer each month. Wadworth 6X, IPA, Farmers Glory and Old Timer, Hall and Woodhouse Tanglefoot, Badger Best Bitter and Bunces Best Bitter are the regular brews. Also available on draught are John Smiths Bitter, Castlemaine XXXX, Red Stripe, Traditional Taunton Dry Scrumpy, Dry Blackthorn cider and Autumn Gold. Prices are very reasonable.

It is very refreshing to walk into a pub and not be knocked back by the smell of stale fried food. Food is limited to good snacks like ploughman's, homemade pasties £1 and filled rolls from 80p.

There is a safe enclosed garden with swings, climbing frame and a slide. Adult activities include darts, dominoes, quiz nights, cricket, fishing, shooting and petanque. There is impromptu folk music on Friday evenings and well behaved dogs are welcome in the bar.

The pub is open 11.30 - 14.30 and 18.00 - 23.00, all day Saturday and the normal Sunday hours.

Lymington Road, East End. Tel (01590) 65223   * "Don't Miss" award

Built as a pub in 1825, the East End Arms is one of the last "real" Forest pubs and promises to stay that way. It was bought by one of the world's greatest rock bands, certainly my favourite, with the aim of ensuring that it would never become a plastic, open-plan pub serving mass produced food to indiscerning grockles. There is a splendid, traditional public bar with original stone floor and real fire and a lounge bar, less authentic but also with an open fire and pine tables for diners. The decor is uncluttered and both the locals and landlord Dave Haywood, are extremely friendly and sure to entertain you with stories about the hamlet. East End is signposted from Buckler's Hard and from the Beaulieu to Lymington Road.

A popular free house dispensing an excellent selection of up to twelve real ales straight from the wood. Brews may include Hook Norton Best Bitter, Fullers London Pride, Ringwood Fortyniner, Morland Old Speckled Hen, Adnams Broadside and Cooks Yardarm. Also on draught are Whitbread Best Bitter, Guinness, Mild, Carlsberg, Carlsberg Export, Dry Blackthorn and Inches Scrumpy cider. Beers are 10p. cheaper in the public bar!

The pub specialises in locally made pies and game but also offers a good local menu listed on the blackboard. Dishes include half a pint of prawns £3.00, sausage, egg and chips £3.30, ploughman's £3.00, salmon steak and salad £5.80, filled jacket potatoes from £2.20 and, steak and Guinness or rabbit, hare or venison pies with vegetables and potatoes all £4.95. Traditional puddings include spotted dick, treacle and custard pudding, mud pie and rice pudding, all from £2.00.

There is piped background music and a piano sing-a-long every other Wednesday. Traditional pub games like darts, crib, shove halfpenny and quoites are played. Children are allowed in the bars up to 19.30 but there is also a nice garden. Dogs are welcome inside. Opening hours are from 11.30 - 15.00 and 18.00 - 23.00 and normal Sunday hours.

THE ELM TREE INN 28

Hightown Road, Hightown, near Ringwood. Tel (01425) 472516

The Elm Tree is a delightful, thatched, country inn on the borders of the New Forest. Originally a 17th century farmhouse and barn, the character has been retained but the buildings have been converted into a large inn with two function rooms. The attractive rural bar features brick and beams with pictures of country scenes and has a well stocked bookcase. The pub is managed by Mike and Kate Lawton and assistant manager, Martin.

The pub is owned by Whitbread and up to eight real ales are served including Fremlins Bitter, Winter Royal, Wadworth 6X, Flowers Original and a regular guest ale. Whitbread Best Bitter, Murphys stout, Stella Artois, Heineken, Heineken Export and Strongbow cider are also served on draught.

The dining area is very attractive with old bricks and beams, a large open fireplace and a smoking loft, which was formerly used for baking bread and smoking ham. The menu has something to cater for all tastes and is reasonably priced, with meals being served all day, every day. Starters include crispy mushrooms £1.95, fresh salads from £3.65, followed by homemade steak and kidney pie with chipped or jacket potatoes and vegetable of the day £3.75, jumbo sausage and fried egg £2.95, and a range of daily specials such as jacket wedges served with garlic and chive dip £1.80 and mushroom and nut fettucine served with a side salad £4.50. Vegetarian dishes are always available.

The Barn Function Room seats 100 people and is decorated with old agricultural implements, (charge £15, £25 at weekends). The Forest Room is a well equipped room available for private business meetings, (charge £10).

There is a pleasant garden and a large car park. Opening hours are from 11.00 - 23.00 Monday to Saturday and food is served all day Sunday, although the bar is only open the normal hours.

THE FAMOUS BLACK CAT

Queen Street, Lymington. Tel (01590) 672139

The Black Cat, formerly the Old English Gentleman, looks deceptively unexciting from the roadside frontage, but the interior is designed in the traditional English concept typical of a Devenish Greenall property. The pub area is spacious but still cosy with low, dark beams, a real fire and old photographs. The original cellar has been converted into the "pit" and makes an intimate dining area with its red-checked table cloths and smoking ban. There is a black cat in residence and also a paw print in a wall brick; possibly the pub ghost?

Four real ales - Marston's Pedigree, Flowers Original, Boddington's Bitter and a guest brew - are served on handpump and Bentley's Yorkshire Biter, Newquay Steam Bitter, Murphys stout, Heineken, Stella Artois, Newquay Steam Pils and Strongbow cider are also available on draught.

Managers, Robert and Linda Hall are both chefs and offer a very reasonably priced menu with such starters as, soup of the day £1.25, prawn cocktail £2,15 and crunchy coated mushrooms £1.95. Main courses include homemade steak and kidney pie £3.25, crispy bacon and cheese baguette £2.65, breast of chicken New Yorker £4.95, crispy coated chicken Kiev £3.25, wholetail scampi £3.75 and rump steak £4.25. There is also a specials board concentrating on fresh local seafood - seafood pasta £3.50, goujons of plaice £4.95 and lemon sole £5.50, - plus a traditional Sunday roast lunch £3.95 and a pensioner's two-course meal from the menu £2.95. Puddings include apple pie, strawberry gâteau and banana split, all £1.95.

The Black Cat is open from 11.00 - 15.00 and 18.00 - 23.00 with normal Sunday hours. Live music every Thursday night and most Sundays, trivia quiz, bar billiards and discos; at other times there is piped music and juke box. Children and dogs are very welcome and there is a mother's and babies room with a disabled toilet and highchairs for younger diners. The car park is at the rear.

THE FILLY INN

Lymington Road, Setley, near Brockenhurst. Tel (01590) 23449

* "Don't Miss" award

The Filly is a splendid old New Forest Inn with low beams, polished brass, lots of forest bits and pieces, and being close to the sea, fishing tackle. The pub's motto, "renowned for good food, fine ales and olde worlde charm" says it all.

A plaque above the bar reads "You come as a stranger but once" and that is how owners Lynn and Tony Bargrove would like you to feel.

This free house offers a good range of ales and features in the Good Beer Guide. Real ales include Ringwood Old Thumper, Wadworth 6X, Draught Bass and Stones Best Bitter. Toby Bitter, Carling Black Label, Kronenbourg, and Dry Blackthorn cider are also on draught. Incidentally, beer prices have decreased by 10 pence in 1994.

The excellent and extensive menu does not change, except for the specials and vegetarian board. Both bar snacks and substantial home-cooked meals are available and reasonably priced. Stilton and garlic burger £2.95, jacket potato filled with garlic mushrooms £2.95, homemade steak and mushroom pie £4.75, Cumberland sausage £4.75, lasagne £3.95, steaks from £7.95, and from the vegetarian board, parsnip and lentil bake, salad and fries for £4.50. We particularly liked the note inviting adults with a smaller appetite to choose from the children's menu. Meals are served every day and you can sit anywhere in the 150 year old bar or the spacious extension. The wine list, with bottles from £6.75, classifies the wines on a sweetness and lightness scale to help your selection.

The pub is a popular venue for a number of clubs, namely running clubs, as landlord Tony is a keen marathon runner, and a wildlife group whose various sculls and nests have often cleared non-members from the group's private corner. This group meets every Tuesday at 20.00 to discuss conservation and to classify specimens.

There is a "Legend of the Fillie Inne" which you can read in full on the back of the menu and offers a possible explanation for the ghost that haunts the pub. The landlord is in no doubt that there is a ghost as all the family has felt it following them and even spoken to it thinking it to be someone present. His daughter says it is the fat man that sits on the end of her bed. Rather than being a highwayman, it is thought to be a previous landlord because he seems so familiar with the original layout of the pub, walking through walls where doors once were.

Opening hours are from 11.00 - 14.30 and 18.30 - 23.00, and normal Sunday hours. We recommend that you don't leave this out of your New Forest itinerary.

THE FISHERMAN'S REST   31

All Saint's Road, Lymington. Tel (01590) 678931

Affectionately known as "The Fish" by the yachties who frequent this old smugglers haunt, this local pub is popular with both young and old. In 1851 the house was called Grattens Cottage and there is a plaque in the pub listing the landlords back to 1870 when 3 gallon kegs were used for smuggling. There is a stone floor, beams, window seats, charts on the walls - and a strong nautical theme including a massive transom plate at the end of the restaurant area, which undoubtably came from an Admirals barge in the 1800's.

This is a free house run by normally absentee landlady Eva Barry who serves real ales - Ringwood Best Bitter, Marston's Pedigree, Wadworth 6X, Flowers Original, Courage Directors and Cooks Yardarm Special Bitter on handpump. Also on draught are Whitbread Best, Guinness, Fosters, Stella Artois, Newquay Steam Pils and Strongbow cider.

The bar menu over the gas fireplace lists homemade soup £2.40, half-a-pint of prawns £2.95, homemade burgers from £3.95, bellie buster jumbo sausage in a baguette £2.20 and sirloin steak sandwich for £3.95. More substantial dishes appear on the blackboard menu and may include home-cooked pies such as cottage pie £4.50 and game pie £5.95 spaghetti bolognaise £4.75, curry and poppadoms £4.75, steak and kidney pie £5.40, ploughman's from £3.25, seafood platter £4.50, plaice and chips £4.90, fisherman's pie £5.95, dressed crab salad £7.50, moules mariniére £6.95 and charcoal grilled fillet steak £11.95. Desserts include spotted dick, apricot crumble, apple tart with cream or custard, treacle tart and toffee and pecan pie, all £2.50.

The Fish is open 11.00 - 15.00 and 17.30 - 23.00 Monday to Friday, Saturday all day and normal Sunday hours. Happy hour and a half is from 17.30 till 19.00 Monday to Friday. Children and dogs are welcome inside and there is a patio area but no garden. Credit cards accepted.

Godshill, Fordingbridge. Tel (01425) 652462

Beware of the sheep! They don't just stray across the road in front of the pub, they sleep in it! The Godshill area is not short of history - the oldest pond in the Forest, stocked with Lung fish, is close by, as is the site of the cock fighting ring which is still visible and a Roman site overlooking the Avon at Frankenbury. The Fighting Cocks is a family run pub built in 1927 overlooking the forest and features a large through bar with a large brick fireplace and flowers on the tables in the adjoining family area. The atmosphere is friendly and the staff and licensee Joyce Harrison will make you welcome. It is pleasing to see clean glasses, hand washed and dried, without that inevitable machine washed rim! The pub is a popular haunt for locals in the winter season, and because of its location, for tourists in the summer.

This popular Whitbread house offers Flowers Original, Wadworth 6X, and guest ales, such as Greene King Abbot Ale, Ringwood Best or Fortyniner on handpump. In addition, Whitbread Best Bitter, Mild, Guinness, Heineken, Stella Artois and Strongbow cider are on draught.

The food is good and includes sandwiches from £1.50, prawn cocktail £2.95, pâté and toast £2.95, ploughman's from £3.25, beef curry £4.75, chilli con carne £4.75, lasagne verdi £4.95, steak and kidney pie £4.50, and salads. Evening specials include steaks from £6.95, mixed grill £7.75, plaice thermidor £5.95, chicken Kiev £5.75 and chicken cordon bleu £5.75. The specials board may list a generous chicken leg, salad and fries £3.95 and cottage pie £4.95. Desserts include fabulous chocolate fudge cake and cream, apple pie and Louisiana lovebite all £1.75. Children have their own menu from £1.75.

The Fighting Cocks is open 11.00 - 15.00 and 18.00 - 23.00 weekdays and the normal Sunday hours. Dogs are welcome inside.

Overnight caravans are catered for and coaches are welcome.

The Bridges, Ringwood. Tel (01425) 473185

Drop off the Ringwood bypass and you will find youself in the car park of the Fish Inn, an attractive, 300-year-old thatched pub that nestles beside the River Avon offering budget meals and boasts, what must be the most cluttered walls in the Forest. Licensee, Mike Nash, modestly called it junk but there is an incredible collection of over 300 plates, Singer sewing machines, fishing tackle and obscene postcards. It should be seen. The interior has cosy, prettily decorated rooms, an open fire and those intimate corners for that illicite affair. One of our favourite touches was the "quote of the week" blackboard. At the beginning of March Mark Twain was featured. "Part of the secret of success in life is to eat and drink what you like and let it fight it out inside".

Owned by Whitbread it offers four real ales - Brakspear Bitter, Flowers Original, Boddingtons Bitter, Ringwood Old Thumper - on handpump and also Whitbread Best Bitter, Murphys stout, Heineken, Stella Artois and Dry Blackthorn cider on draught. Reasonably priced house wine.

There is an extensive menu, a daily specials board, a no-smoking dining area, children's corner - highchair available - three-course meals from £10 per couple and senior citizen's two-course lunches £2.95. Dishes include sandwiches from £1.75, egg mayonnaise with prawns £2.95, calamares £2.20, Atlantic prawn cocktail £2.95, sirloin steak in French bread £3.25, crusty bread platters from £2.95, beef and ale pie £4.95, venison in port and cranberry sauce £4.95, lamb and mint pie £4.95 and a brunch grill from the chargrill £4.95.

The Fish Inn is open all day in the summer season, otherwise 11.00 - 15.00 and 17.30 - 23.00 and the normal Sunday hours. Attractive riverside lawn with children's play area. Live folk and country music on Thursday nights, otherwise piped music fills the bar. No electronic games and no dogs inside. Credit cards accepted. Good large car park.

Winkton, near Christchurch. Tel (01202) 477283

Dating back to 1673 this country house appears more of a hotel restaurant but there is a friendly pub style bar with an original well with continuously running spring water. Various local handicrafts hang on the walls and are offered for sale.

The Fisherman's Haunt is a free house with Ringwood Best Bitter, Fortyniner and Bass on handpump. Also on draught are Toby Bitter, Stones Best Bitter, John Smiths, Worthington Best Bitter, McEwans Export, Carling Black Label, Becks Bier, Tennent's Extra, Fosters, Carlsberg lager, Guinness, Taunton Autumn Gold and Dry Blackthorn cider.

This is a popular eating place with servery and average priced bar snacks from a fairly typical pub menu. The specials board includes homemade pies and ribs. Pub menu; homemade soup of the day £1.60, home-cooked ham, two fried eggs and chips £4.30, two pork and beef sausages, onion rings, chips and peas £3.20, fried fillet of fresh plaice, chips and peas £4.25, scampi, chips and peas £4.50, toasted sandwich cheese and onion £2.10, and cheese and ham £2.50, ploughman's from £3.50 and roast of the day £4.75. Assorted sweets, gateaux, ice creams and homemade pies from £2.00. Children's menu including fish fingers, chips and baked beans plus ice cream from £2.75. The restaurant menu includes a three course set menu at £10.95 with such dishes as rump steak, chicken and trout. But special requests are catered for.

The bar is open 10.30 - 14.30 Monday to Friday (10.30 - 15.00 Saturday) and 18.00 - 23.00. Normal Sunday hours. Accommodation from £32 single and £54 double (£63 with four-poster and en-suite bathroom). Egon Ronay recommended. Dogs can be accommodated.

Pilley, near Lymington. Tel (01590) 672158

* "Don't Miss" award
* "Good Food" award

Originally a pair of Forester's cottages - the tree roots and fireplace opening can still be seen in the stone flagged entrance - this is the oldest pub in the Forest and as you enter you will see a list of landlords dating back to 1498. In fact records show that beer has been sold on the premises since the time of William the Conqueror, who owned much of the Forest and whose coat-of-arms included a Fleur-de-Lys. The pub is delightful, cottage style with low ceilings, brick walls, wooden beams, a massive open fire place and the most spectacular sparkling copper that you will see in the Forest. The character is genuine, there are two cosy bars and a tastefully decorated dining room. The Jacob Armitage and Beverly of Arnwood bars are named after characters from the book "The Children of the New Forest" written in the locality, and the Inn is also described in Sir Arthur Conan-Doyle's book, "The White Company".

Craig Smallwood runs the pub on a long lease from Whitbreads, dispensing Whitbread Best Bitter, Boddingtons, Wadworth 6X, Flowers Original, Old Speckled Hen, Ringwood Best, Heineken and Stella Artois.

The food is excellent, medium priced, unquestionably value-for-money and specialising in venison, rabbit and other local catches. The menu includes Ardennes pâté with hot brown toast £3.25, chicken fillets with asparagus £6.95, grilled swordfish steak £7.95, greenlip mussels £4.75, Fleur De Lys special salad £4.85, herb sausage £3.95, sweets from £2.50 include a huge strawberry pavlova, BBQ's and special evenings. Until a few years ago ham was smoked in the chimney and the chain and pulley can still be seen in the chimney head.

Open from 11.00 - 15.00 and 17.30 - 23.00. Sunday 12.00 - 15.00 and 19.00 - 22.30. Access, Switch and Visa accepted.

FLYING BOAT INN 36

Calshot Beach, Calshot. Tel (01703) 893439

This is the largest pub in the South, set on a five acre sight and previously the officers mess for the Royal Air Force. Origins of the RAF in Calshot date back to 1912 when they were established to defend the coastal waters. All that is left now is the wartime memorabilia that adorns the walls of the Flying Boat Inn. As you head towards Calshot Activity Centre you will see this unusual white and pink building on your right. There is a function room for weddings, exhibitions and reunions and a late night licence till 02.00. The bar is large and joins a restaurant area and games bar with skittle alley at the rear.

The flying boat is a freehouse owned by Betty Clibbon. Real ales are Flowers Original and Strong Country Bitter, with Whitbread Best Bitter, Mild, Guinness, Heineken, Carlsberg Export, Autumn Gold and Dry Blackthorn cider also on draught. Thursday evening 20p off every pint!

Pub grub ordered from the blackboard at the servery is wholesome, value for money food and includes sandwiches from £1, soup of the day £1.50, cottage pie £3.50, ploughman's £2.50, lasagne at £3.50, steak and kidney pie £3.50, braised beef and onion £3.50, scampi £4.00, gammon, ham and egg £4.00, mixed grill £4.00, rump steak with all the trimmings £6.50 and vegetarian meals £3.50. There is a Sunday carvery and a children's menu.

Credit cards, Visa, Amex and Access are accepted but not encouraged. There is pool, dartboard, skittle alley and a video jukebox in the games bar. The Flying Boat is open 11.00 - 15.00 and 19.00 - 23.00 with normal Sunday hours.

THE FORESTERS ARMS 37

10, Brookley Road, Brockenhurst. Tel (01590) 23397

The Foresters Arms is a traditional, family run pub, originally a blacksmith's forge, with two quite distinct bars decorated with caricatures of the regulars and pictures of Brockenhurst in bygone days. The lounge bar is cosy and comfortable and has been recently enlarged to avoid the summer spill over onto the pavement. The "public" Forest bar has often been described as raucous. However, there is a very friendly atmosphere and a good mix of customers.

Peter and Jackie Murray run this Whitbread pub partnership offering real ales - Ringwood Best Bitter, Boddingtons Bitter and Wadworth 6X on handpump also Whitbread Best, Guinness, Murphys stout, Stella Artois and Strongbow cider.

The Foresters prides itself on its reputation for homemade meals, especially pies, at reasonable prices and we noted the portions were generous. Snacks featured are sandwiches from £2 and toasties from £3. Starters: garlic mushrooms with dip £2.50, pâté and toast £2.75 and prawn cocktail £2.75. Main meals are served with potatoes and fresh vegetables and include cheese, ham or tuna salad £4.25, roast of the day £4.50 and fillet of sole with scallops and crabmeat £5.50. Typical dishes listed on the specials board are marinated rabbit £4.75, steak and kidney pudding £4.75 and tuna and asparagus lasagne £4.50. Vegetarians are well catered for - lentil and potato bake, and nut roast both £4 and sweets £2 include sherry trifle, chocolate swirl cheesecake and bread and butter pudding. Varied children's menu for those under ten, and highchair available.

The toilets are refreshingly clean and there is a very small garden and a delightful patio area where you can watch the world go by.

Open all day, 11.00 - 23.00 weekdays and normal Sunday opening hours. Last food orders 14.30 and 21.00. Dogs welcome in the public bar only.

Frogham, near Fordingbridge. Tel (01425) 652294   * "Real Ale" award

At the end of a maize of attractive, narrow, twisty and surprisingly steep Forest lanes you will find the Foresters Arms. Built around the turn of the century, it is a friendly, family run free house. It is certainly a traditional, unspoilt, local pub with an open fire, plastered walls, a thatched bar, and with old photographs, antlers, farm tools and saws adorning the walls. There is also a family dining area as well as an airy games room overlooking a well kept garden.

The pub is renowned for its well kept real ales and serves up to 150 different brews every year. Draught Bass and Boddingtons Bitter are always available with regular guest ales like Ringwood Porter, Craftsman Traditional Premium Ale, Theakston XB and Everards Old Original. Murphys stout, Heineken, Stella Artois and Dry Blackthorn cider are also served on draught.

The Foresters is also known for its good food and generous helpings. The wide ranging menu includes light bites such as garlic mushrooms, smoked mackerel both £2.95 and giant Mediterranean prawns and garlic bread £5.75. Fish dishes include local Avon trout £6.95, deep fried fillet of plaice £4.75 and deep fried breaded scampi £5.45. Other main course choices range from chargrill steaks from £8.95, Murphys steak and mushroom pie £5.45, chicken curry £4.95 and half a chicken and chips £7.25 to a traditional lasagne £4.95. A specials board lists fresh mussels in season. Omelettes, salads, ploughman's and children's dishes £1.95, are also available. Puddings from £1.50 include gâteau of the day, apple pie, cheesecake and sherry trifle.

The Foresters Arms is open 11.00 - 14.30 (15.00 Saturday) and 18.00 - 23.00 and normal Sunday hours. Horses are welcome as are children, and dogs on leads. Pool, darts, fruit machine and juke box. Watch out for the popular beer festivals with at least 20 real ales to sample. Credit cards accepted. Camping nearby.

THE FOREST HEATH HOTEL   39

Station Road, Sway. Tel (01590) 682287

Originally a Victorian coaching inn, this is a friendly, local village pub with two bars, a louder public with pool, darts and regular live music, and a quieter lounge with old photographs, reference books above the bar and adjoining restaurant.

Recommended by CAMRA, this free house offers an admirable choice of real ales including Forest Heath Bitter, Boddingtons, Pompey Royal, Arthur Pendragon Strong Beer, Smiles Best and Wadworth 6X.

Traditional pub food is medium priced at around £5 for a main course. A la carte lunchtime and evening menu available in the restaurant.

The Forest Heath opens 11.00 - 15.00 and 18.00 - 23.00 Monday to Friday and all day Saturday and in the summer season. Sunday normal hours. Secure children's play area, petanque and accommodation including the same for pets. Credit cards accepted.

THE FOREST INN   40

Lyndhurst Road, Ashurst. Tel (01703) 292331

You will feel at home as soon as you walk into the Forest Inn, as it is an unpretentious, traditional pub with what my partner described as having a convivial atmosphere. There is a spacious main bar with open log fires, piped music and a pleasant eating area where one will be given a warm welcome from managers Gill and Ed Crowther. The pub interior has recently been refurbished and decorated with various horse brasses, farming tackle and general nick-nacks. Even the beams have numerous witticisms chalked upon them. The nearby butterfly farm with its indoor tropical jungle, is well worth a visit.

Although this is a Whitbread managed house there is a good selection of real ales on offer, for example Morland Old Speckled Hen, Ringwood Best Bitter, Wadworth 6X, Flowers Original and Wethereds Winter Royal. Murphys stout, Heineken, Stella Artois and Strongbow cider are also on draught. Gales Country wines sold by the glass.

The blackboard menu changes all the time and may feature cod and chips £3.45, steak and kidney pie £3.95, faggots, mushy peas and mashed potato £3.50, cauliflower cheese with jacket potato £4.25, Cumberland toad in the hole £4.25 and scampi and chips £4.75. Sweets include apple and sultana pudding, chocolate fudge gâteau, chocolate sponge and spotted dick from £2.25. Sunday roast £4.50. In the summer there is a top value breakfast priced from £1.50 according to your appetite. Last food orders on Sunday at 21.00.

The bar is open all day 11.00 - 23.00 weekdays and normal Sunday hours. Children, but not dogs, are allowed in the pub if they are accompanied by adults eating. Good large garden with bouncey castle for energetic children. Piano music on Thursday nights, barbecue site for hire and ferret racing in the summer. Credit cards accepted.

Rhinefield Road, Brockenhurst. Tel (01590) 22844

If you are nervous of entering hotel bars, don't be. This little gem is a real pub inside an excellent hotel and has the added bonus of serving the cheapest beer in the Forest. Originally a vicarage built on a Forest site granted by the crown, Forest Park became a hotel in 1902. Although a little off the beaten track it is close to the picturesque Rhinefield Drive and offers top facilities. The pub is intimate with settles and beams, and decorated with football scarves and rugby programmes.

At the time of visiting (August '94) Whitbread Best Bitter (£1.10), Ringwood Fortyniner, Ushers Founders Ale and Whitchwood Dog's Bollocks (6.5%) were on handpump. Heineken, Heineken Export and Scrumpy Jack cider were also on draught.

Bar snacks include ploughman's from £2.95, jacket potatoes from £2.55, toasted sandwiches £3.25, ham salad platter £4.95, pasta of the day £3.95, Forest Park grill £3.95, steak sandwich £4.95 and New Forest sausages £4.50.

The pub is open all day 11.00 - 23.00 with normal Sunday hours. Dogs, children and credit cards welcome. Jukebox and plenty of garden. Bed and breakfast accommodation from £42.95 single and £32.95 per person double.

Lyndhurst. Tel (01703) 282098

This is a family orientated pub recently taken over by Tom and Vikki Miles who are aiming at offering a well managed, value for money, outlet. The bar is spacious yet cosy, partitioned by beams and with reproduction pictures and branding irons decorating the walls. Originally an old coaching inn on the Bournemouth to London route, the stables were at the back. More recently, as the name suggests, the local hunt used to meet at the pub.

A Whitbread pub it offers Whitbread Best Bitter, Guinness, Murphys stout, Heineken, Stella Artois, Strongbow and Max Dry (6%) cider on draught, plus real ales Whitbread Winter Royal, Boddingtons Bitter, Flowers Original and Marston's Pedigree on handpump. good selection of wines from £7 per bottle.

There is a daily specials board, and separate lunch and evening menus which are divided up into produce from the sea, fields, pond, coop, garden and from the poacher. Hors d'oeuvres can be selected from the starters bar and the fish is fresh. Dishes include hot chilli tacos and melted cheese £2.25, pan fried tuna steak in garlic butter £5.95, 12oz lemon sole £6.95, rainbow trout pan fried in herb butter with almonds and stuffed with prawns £6.45, salmon en croute £7.99, lamb chops £5.95, slices of duck breast in orange sauce £7.50 and jugged hare cooked in a gravy of ale and onions £5.45. Good selection of vegetables, two-course Sunday roast £5.99 and a three-course "golden years" menu £5.99. Sweets £1.95 include homemade rhubarb crumble, lemon cheesecake, sticky toffee gâteau and chocolate fudge gâteau. Food is served up to 22.00.

The Fox and Hounds is open all day - 11.00 - 23.00 - weekdays and the normal Sunday hours. There is a local's area with dartboard, children's area away from the bar, a pretty patio garden and dogs are welcome inside. Fox Pot challenge every Tuesday at 20.00. Tea, coffee and breakfasts are served from 10.00.

Woodlands Road, Near Ashurst. Tel (01703) 293093   * "Management" award

Some landlords can be accused of being indifferent about the services they offer. Paul Hingston is certainly not one of these. At the Gamekeeper you will find a good range of beers and wines and an innovative atmosphere. The pub is located in a quiet village lane at Woodlands between Bartley, Ashurst and Netley Marsh. It was fairly recently refurbished but it still maintains its traditional feel with beams, a real fire, piano, matches in a brick on the bar and forest bric-a-brac, tools and stuffed birds. It is a well managed popular pub, built around 1880 by Strong's. Previously named the Royal Oak and of somewhat dubious reputation, this pub has really been turned around for the better. As a free house some unusual beers are on offer. Real ales may include Ruddles, HSB, Pots Ale and Websters. John Smiths, Mild, Guinness, Kronenbourg, Carlsberg, Fosters and Strongbow cider are on draught. There is also a complete range of Gales Country wines including Birch, and the moreish, Strawberry.

All the food is prepared and cooked on the premises and sweets are homemade by the two chefs. Starters include whitebait and garlic mushrooms, both at £1.95. "County Fayre" includes Norfolk jumbo sausages and egg £4.25 and half a BBQ chicken at £5.75. Other main courses include steak and Guinness pie £4.25, salmon steak £6.50, Gamekeepers grill £7.95 and 16oz T-bone steak at £10.95. A specials board includes cottage pie £4.50 and rack of ribs with hickory sauce £6.95. Sunday roast £4.50. Sweets £2.25 include banoffee pie, stawberry cheese-cake, nutty treacle tart, lemon syllabub and white chocolate mousse. All children's dishes are £1.95. A high chair is available.

There is a narrow garden with climbing frames for children who are also allowed in the dining area and the conservatory. There is a popular quiz every Sunday, karaoke and various special events including a beach party, Monday bric-a-brac auction and BBQ in the pub!

The Gamekeeper is open 11.00 - 14.30 and 18.00 - 23.00 from Monday to Friday, all day Saturday and normal Sunday hours.

GEORGE HOTEL 44

Market Place, Ringwood. Tel (01425) 474163

Situated in the centre of Ringwood, the George is a young, lively, informal town pub on split levels. The decor is unpretentious with beams and a refreshing lack of clutter.

This is a Whitbread pub with Tetley Best Bitter and Burton Ale on handpump. Whitbread Best Bitter, Guinness, Heineken, Stella Artois and Olde English cider are also on draught.

The food is reasonably priced and includes starters from £1.35, steak and mushroom pie £3.50, seafood platter £3.50, vegetable moussaka £2.25 and gammon steak £3.50.

The George Hotel is open all day 10.00 - 23.00 and normal Sunday hours. Accommodation available.

THE GEORGE INN 45

Bridge Street, Fordingbridge. Tel (01425) 652040

The George is noted for its stunning position close to the River Avon, its attractive patio flanks the river's edge and fish can be seen easily in the clear water. Inside there is an uncluttered bar with wooden flooring, and a separate dining area with the classic Wayside Inns decor.

Since Fordingbridge was once a centre for smugglers, it is not suprising that the George is mentioned in several historic accounts. The most famous smuggler was Captain Diamond, "The Smuggler King" and there were many fights between his men and the Customs and Excise men. After a bloody battle on the site of the George Inn, Diamond escaped to Whitsbury but was betrayed, arrested and hanged at Deadman's Corner nearby. The George was also used as a lookout by gamekeepers to observe poachers entering Fordingbridge over the only bridge from the forest.

It is a Whitbread property managed by Alex Crisp who serves six real ales, including Marston's Pedigree, Wadworth 6X, Boddingtons Bitter and Flowers Original. Whitbread Best, Murphys stout, Heineken, Stella Artois and Strongbow cider are also available on draught.

The George is a food orientated pub with a specials board highlighting home-made pies and pasta. The main menu is very reasonably priced with 'lite' bites including a fresh granary cob filled with prawns and served with chips £2.99, and "hot" bites such as a 4oz sirloin with fries £2.45. Hearty meals include sausage, mash and beans £3.45 and traditional fish, chips and peas £3.75.

Children are allowed in the conservatory and dining area. Dogs are not allowed. Credit cards are accepted.

Opening hours are 11.00 to 23.00 Monday to Saturday, normal Sunday hours.

GLEN EAGLES 46

Butts Ash Lane, Hythe. Tel (01703) 842162

Originally called the Jester when it was opened by Strong's in 1961, it was renamed in 1986 after the famous golfing hotel. This "back to front" pub, backs onto the road and is fronted with a quiet, well kept garden filled with the sound of pigeons and attractions for children, including a trampoline and a tree house.

As one would expect the interior is adorned with golfing memorabilia collected over the years by licencee, Geoff Mercer. Decor is plush, but slightly tired, red velvet, with an open fire, beams and unusual collection of teapots.

It boasts a local trade and considers itself a "family" pub. Owned by Whitbread the pub offers four real ales - Strong Country Bitter, Flowers Original, Wadworth 6X, Ringwood Best Bitter, Whitbread Best Bitter, Whitbread, Murphys stout, Heineken, Stella Artois and Strongbow cider are also available on draught.

At lunchtime an extensive menu lists the selection of good value, home-cooked bar meals, many of which are under £4.50. Choices include sandwiches from £1.65, toasted torpedo rolls from £1.85, pâté campagne £1.95, seafood dip £2.25, cold fisherman's platter £4.25, tuna salad £4.50, steak and kidney pie, hot spicy chilli both £3.95, deep fried chicken £3.95, sirloin steak £6.95, mixed grill £5.75 and steak au poivre £7.95. Children's dishes £1.50.

The Glen Eagles is open all day 11.00 - 23.00 with normal Sunday hours. "Happy hour" Friday 17.00 to 18.00 and half-hour Sundays 12.00 - 12.30. Facilities for the disabled and a discount card scheme for pensioners, plus live rock, jazz or soul music on Thursdays. Games include darts and petanque. No dogs. Credit cards accepted.

Brook, near Cadnam. Tel (01703) 813359

The Green Dragon is located off junction 1 of the M27. Follow signposts to the tiny hamlet of Brook. The building dates from the 15th century and was originally the premises for a wheelwright and coffin-maker before becoming a beer house some 200 years ago. It is not unusual to see New Forest ponies seeking shade on the forecourt in this delightful rural setting. This is a good local's pub that has not been spoilt through recent refurbishment. There is a comfortable and popular dining area, and The Tack Room; a cosy public bar with horse brasses, an open fire, tiled floor and original beams. Both bars display leather sheets branded with the marks of animal owners who have Commoner's Rights to graze the Forest. Darts and dominoes are played by local leagues.

This is a Whitbread partnership - Doug Swann is your host - offering a good selection of real ales; Morland Old Speckled Hen, Flowers Original, Castle Eden Ale and Boddingtons Bitter. Whitbread Best Bitter, Guinness, Murphys stout, Heineken and Stella Artois are also available on draught.

The lunchtime menu is posted on blackboards and there is a separate evening menu with further specials at the weekend. Popular dishes include homemade steak and kidney pie £5.85 and grilled liver and bacon with creamed potato and fresh vegetables £5.25. Evening starters range from soup of the day £2.00 to smoked fish platter £4.50. Main courses include fillet of salmon marinated in a spicy Mesquite sauce £7.95, breast of chicken Kiev £6.25 and Dragon's mega mix for the very hungry £12.50. There is a vegetarian selection, Sunday roasts and wines from £5.95 a bottle.

Children are welcome away from the bar, dogs at the landlord's discretion and most credit cards. There is a good garden with a heated patio and children's play area. The pub is open 11.00 - 15.00 and 18.00 - 23.00, and the normal Sunday hours.

Keyhaven, near Lymington. Tel (01590) 642391   * "Don't Miss" award

This 17th century pub is situated close to Keyhaven harbour and its popular sailing club. The pub is named after Colonel Hawker's hunting gun which claimed 17753 victims. He resided next door in "Hawker's Cottage". It undoubtably has a ghost, the premises having previously accommodated the ale house, chapel and mortuary. The Gun is very attractive and cosy being decorated with various nautical memorabilia and collections of old matchboxes and cigarette cards. It is popular with the local's, notably the yachting fraternity, and with tourists.

This is a Whitbread partnership run by Paul and Jacqueline Hill. Real ales include Ringwood Fortyniner, Flowers Original, Boddingtons Bitter, Marston's Pedigree, Morland Old Speckled Hen and Brakspear Bitter. Whitbread Best Bitter, Guinness, Heineken, Stella Artois, Murphys stout, Strongbow cider and Autumn Gold are also on draught. Although the Gun tends to be on the expensive side, being the first in the Forest area to cross the £2.00 a pint mark for Stella, we were delighted to find West Country Pale Ale at a mere £1.20 a pint. There are 60 malt whiskies on offer and Gales Country wines.

The food is good with crab and lobster in season. The menu includes prawn or crab sandwiches £2.75, prawn cocktail £2.85, smoked salmon pâté with side salad £2.95, crab pâté £2.95, quarter roast chicken £4.50, garlic battered chicken goujons £4.50, calamari romana £4.50, jacket potato filled with cold water prawns and cocktail sauce £4.00 and local dressed crab in season £5.50. Sweets £1.85. A playing card system marks your turn.

There is a patio room, a delightful snug area for children, and a spacious beer garden with swings. There are summer barbecues and live, folk or country and western music, on Thursday nights.

Opening hours are from 11.00 - 15.00 and 18.00 - 23.00 and the usual Sunday hours. Car parking is at the "Pay and Display" across the road.

Durnstown, Sway. Tel (01590) 682404   *Finalist "Pub of the Year" award

Every journalist's nightmare, the Hare and Hounds does not fit any of the normal cliches such as, "traditional", "village", or "country", to describe a pub. Originally a mortuary some 300 years ago, it is certainly comfortable with a long main bar area and a substantial section made availabe for family dining. Every area is different, one devoted to 1920's and 30's memorabilia and another with library wallpaper, which if it were not for the plastic chairs, would give the allusion of dining in a classic atmosphere. The elegant bow window, welcoming open fires and comfy chairs in the main bar area are the sort you would expect to find in the foyer of a country hotel. However, it has a relaxing, not stuffy ambience; "Feel free to get up and dance" commented licensees Ian and Beverly Crouch, or enjoy the Sunday quiz night.

There is a minimum of four real ales on offer at this Whitbread establishment, West Country Pale Ale, Wadworth 6X, Flowers Original and Morland Old Speckled Hen. Whitbread Best Bitter, Guinness, Murphys stout, Heineken, Stella Artois, Strongbow and Scrumpy Jack ciders are also available on draught.

The menu is no less unusual with some thirty main courses and a separate oriental menu. Dishes include marinated chicken £6.95, BBQ half rack £6.25, lasagne £4.95, basket meals and cod bites £3.50, daily roast £4.95, salmon shanti £6.50 and huge ploughman's from £3.25. The "kiddies corner" menu prices from £2.50 includes a free lollipop.

Facilities at the pub include a babies changing room, a separate dining area for parents and children, a tie up rail for horses and a 56-inch screen to view various sporting events.

Dogs are welcome. Laid back piped music but no fruit machines. There is a large award winning garden and a substantial car park. The bar is open 11.00 - 23.00 Monday to Saturday, normal hours on Sunday.

HAPPY CHEESE 50

189 Lyndhurst Road, Ashurst. Tel (01703) 293232

Once a top class restaurant this is now a popular meeting place for the young at heart from the city. There is plenty of room with many seating areas, family dining area and beer garden. Also darts and fruit machines.

Wooden floors, stone flagging, disabled facilities. Recently refurbished this pub is a "Fork and Pitcher" concept, a traditional British pub, an eaters pub! but still catering to the mass market. There are four open log fires, scatter rugs and beams.

Bass Taverns – four real ales including Bass, Worthington, Draft Ruddles and Caffereys Bitter. Also on draught, Carling Black Label, Guinness and Dry Blackthorn cider.

The menu includes soups £1.50, smoked mackerel £2.50, garlic mushrooms £2.50, steak and kidney pie £4.65 and mixed grill £6.95.

No dogs, children yes. Garden and play equipment. Open 11.00 - 23.00. Sunday normal hours. Most credit cards accepted.

THE HAY WAIN 51

Southampton Road, Bartley, near Cadnam. Tel (01703) 812243

This is a typical, well managed Brewers Fayre property with a large dining area, bar area and garden. The decor is the Laura Ashley look with a tidy bar and brass foot-rails.

Owned by Whitbreads, real ales on offer include Wadworth 6X and Boddingtons Bitter. Also on draught are Whitbread Best, Guinness, Heineken, Heineken Export, Stella Artois, Murphys stout and Strongbow cider.

Food is good value and the standard menu includes farmhouse pâté £1.95, fish dips £2.55, Cajun fingers £2.25, Westmorland pie £4.25, chicken masala £4.95, vegetable crumble £4.95, steak and kidney pie £3.95, chicken escalopes with lemon £4.95, fish pie £4.95, fillet of salmon £5.95, and fresh salad platters from £3.75. Sunday roast £4.95 and hot puddings £1.95. Liqueur coffee only £1.85 and reasonably priced house wine.

The Hay Wain is open all day 11.00 - 23.00 including Sunday for diners. Children are welcome and most major credit cards.

Linwood, near Ringwood. Tel (01425) 473973

The High Corner Inn is tucked away in the heart of the forest at the end of a long, but well maintained gravel track. It is an idyllic and typical country pub but deceptively large with several bars, family rooms, Lego room, public squash courts, restaurant, eight en-suite bedrooms and private facilities for weddings, conferences and barbecues.

Originally a 300-year-old farm house, the building became an hotel for the gentry of London at the turn of the century, a status it retained until the 1960's. Real beams and barrel seats characterise the rambling series of rooms, the main bar being decorated with currency notes collected by landlords Roger and Lin Kernan and donated by customers. The lower bar is adorned with book matches.

It is a popular free house, especially in the summer, serving Whitbread Best Bitter, Marston's Pedigree, Wadworth 6X, Boddingtons Bitter, Murphys stout, Guinness, Stella Artois, Swan Light and Dry Blackthorn cider on draught.

There is a bar snack menu, separate menu for the light and airy Deer's Leap Restaurant. Both menu's are imaginative and reasonably price. The restaurant menu includes smoked fish bouchée blended in white wine sauce served in a puff pastry case £2.85 and Stilton fritters £3.35 followed by roast breast of Barbury duck served with a choice of sauces £7.95 and roast rack of lamb princess at £6.95. Extensive bar snack choices range from warm seasonal salad with croutons and walnut dressing £2.85 and baked local trout with tomato mayonnaise £5.25 to a 7oz. griddled pork chop with barbecue sauce £4.85. Good selection of vegetarian meals, light snacks - ploughman's, sandwiches - plus a children's menu and home-made sweets such as sherry trifle and banana mess £2.50.

Woodland garden with picnic benches and an adventure playground. Disabled facilities and a welcome for dogs on leads. Opening hours are from 11.00 - 14.30 and 18.00 (19.00 in winter) - 23.00 and all day summer Saturdays. Usual licensing hours on Sunday, but all-day carvery. Credit cards accepted.

HEATH HOTEL 53

Beaulieu Road, Dibden Purlieu. Tel (01703) 842275

Predictably Brewers Fayre, this pub on the edge of Dibden Purlieu village and the Forest has recently been refurbished and offers good value food and standard furnishings.

Five real ales are on offer and may include Wadworth 6X, Boddingtons Bitter, Morland Old Speckled Hen, Fremlins Bitter and Whitbread Summer Ale. Whitbread Best, Guinness, Murphys stout, Heineken, Heineken Export, Stella Artois and Strongbow cider are also on draught.

The usual Brewers Fayre menu is on offer with starters of prawn cocktail £2.35, chef's choice of soup £1.20 and combo for two £3.95. Main courses include spinach and Ricotta lasagne £4.45, sirloin steak £7.75, half roast chicken £4.75, steak and mushroom pudding £3.95, fillet of plaice £3.95 and light bites such as Cumberland baguette £2.95. Sunday roast £4.95, children's portion £2.95. Sweets from £1.95.

Opening hours are 11.00 - 23.00 including Sunday for those eating. Dogs are not permitted but children and most credit cards are welcome.

HOGS HEAD IN THE FOREST 54

Long Lane, Hardley, near Fawley. Tel (01703) 842270

Converted from a house into a pub back in 1879, this friendly, simply decorated hostelry is conveniently situated close to the gates of the Fawley refinery and according to their shifts, you may meet a warm cross section of oil workers. The licensees, Ian Clarke and Tracy Warren, have modernised the property, without losing its character. The single bar is partly partitioned from the games area and has basic wooden flooring, sacks on the ceiling and a cosy log burner.

Despite flying the Whitbread flag the pub is noted locally for its real ales, offering five regular changing guest cask ales. Standard beers are Boddingtons Bitter, Wadworth 6X, Morland Old Speckled Hen and Marston's Pedigree Bitter with guest ales like Morland Old Masters, Elgood Wisbeck, Arundel Old Knucker, Arundel Strong Hold and Gibbs Mew Bishops Tipple. Also on draught are Whitbread Best, Poacher, Guinness, Murphys stout, Heineken, Stella Artois and Bulmers Traditional cider. Wide selection of bottled Continental beers and lagers.

There is a good range of reasonably priced bar food; snacks include filled rolls £1.25, steakwich £1.50 and egg and bacon butty £1.50. Main dishes listed on a blackboard behind the bar door include gammon steak £3.90, scampi and chips £3.90, lasagne, salad and fries £3.95, steak and kidney pie £3.75, chilli and rice £3.50, cottage pie £3.45, Hog's Head hotpot and tuna and cheese bake both £3.45 and Mexican pie £3.75. Sweets £1.50 range from rhubarb pie and bread pudding to fruits of the Forest pie. Main meals are served until 21.00, snacks are available later.

Open all day, 11.00 - 23.00 and normal Sunday hours. There is a large garden at the rear with children's entertainment - animals, climbing frame, treehouse swings and the venue for tug of war in season! No dogs or children in the bar. Occasional live music, quiz night alternative Tuesdays, darts, crib, fruit machines, juke box and Sky TV in the public area.

Southampton Road, Battramsley, Lymington. Tel (01590) 23291

       * "Don't Miss" award
       * "Good Food" award

No trip to the New Forest would be complete without a visit to the 300-year-old Hobler which was once a butcher's, baker's and a pub combined. The atmosphere is "Foresty", the food is "wild" and the landlord, Pip Stevens, is a self confessed looney, with an irrepressible sense of fun. The pub has an olde-world charm with beams and cosy corners, a library, a gun room with stuffed animals, china, saws and photos of half-naked people stuck around the bar. It is the sort of place where anything might happen so don't be the slightest bit surprised to see a horse or emu walk into the bar. There is an old baker's oven at one end of the main bar area. Nice little touches include free matches and money collected in the urinals!

The real ales change regularly, but expect the selection to include Wadworth 6X, Flowers Original, Moorheads Masters and Smiles Exhibition, as well as Whitbread Best Bitter, Guinness, Heineken, Stella Artois and Strongbow cider.

Not surprisingly the pub has won several awards for its food. The extensive menu is imaginative, the helpings are generous and the menu is covered in graffiti and jokes. The pub is extremely popular so do book if you want an assured table. Dishes include spicy sausages on french bread with fried onions and garnish £2.95, garlic bread with cheese and prawns £3.50, l'escargot cooked in loads of garlic butter £2.50, Hobler hock, a "smallish" joint of pork roasted with a cider and apple sauce £5.95, a rich and creamy fish soup with croutons and rouille with crusty bread £3.95 and chicken satay £4.50. Pip has recently introduced an additional, innovative and more European style of cooking at the table on hot rocks, and fondues. Well priced wine and a good range of malt whiskies.

Opening hours are 11.00 - 14.30 and 18.00 - 23.00 and normal Sunday hours. Excellent spacious garden with summer bar, children's play area and a paddock which is home to many animals. Dogs are not allowed in the bar.

Woodgreen, near Fordingbridge. Tel (01725) 510739

* "PUB OF THE YEAR" award

Don't miss this very friendly village pub. The Horse and Groom quickly fills with locals on opening, drawn by the two cosy, beamed bars, each with warming open fires. Apart from the warm atmosphere there are such delightful touches as matches in a brick on the bar for your use. The building is over a hundred years old, and was once used as stables before becoming a welcoming pub with a rustic, forest decor and a character all of its own. There are plans to build an extension but this will remain in the style of the main building.

Now a free house, real ales include Draught Bass, Flowers Original, Wadworth 6X and Ringwood Best Bitter. Guinness, Carlsberg Pilsner, Carlsberg Export and Stonehouse cider are also available on draught.

The pub offers light bites such as sandwiches £1.15, ploughman's £2.25 and jacket potatoes from £1.80. The main menu offers some very inviting dishes, a little different than the standard pub fayre. Starters include asparagus in a creamy white sauce £2.45 and whitebait £2.25. Main courses feature grills such as Avon trout £5.25, 10oz gammon steak £5.75 and Groom grill with steak, lamb chop, gammon, kidney, liver and sausage £7.95. Deep fries include chicken Kiev £4.95 and turkey nuggets filled with cheese and garlic £4.95. The specials board may list crispy fried Camembert £2.95, steak and kidney pudding £4.50, roast pigeon stuffed with savoury rice £4.50, faggots chips and peas £4.25, half a roast chicken £4.50 and plaice stuffed with prawns and mushrooms for £5.25. Sunday roast at £4.75, plus children's dishes and a sweets board.

The pub boasts a splendid garden with a well stocked aviary and several small domestic animals to keep children amused, plus an area where you can play petanque. Dogs are welcome in the bar. Bed and breakfast nearby.

Opening hours are 11.00 - 15.00 and 18.00 - 23.00 with normal Sunday hours. Outside functions are catered for.

THE HOLBURY   57

Long Lane, Holbury, near Fawley. Tel (01703) 243292

The Holbury is a spacious pub lacking in character but, according to licensee Grace Patterson, "the staff are pleasant and willing to please". It is a real pub, by which we mean it smells of beer not greasy chips, indeed it does not serve any food.

Owned by Whitbread and Solent Inns, the Holbury does however boast the cheapest prices in the area; Whitbread Best Bitter £1.38, Flowers Original £1.51, Murphys £1.72, Guinness £1.73, Heineken £1.52, Stella Artois £1.75, Strongbow cider £1.54 and all liquors at £1.07. (Prices correct December '94)

Almost at the end of the Fawley road, just before the turning to Lepe, the Holbury is a local, two-bar pub. The public bar is a lively games bar with two pool tables, darts, dominoes, cribbage, fruit machine, video games and there is room for a television and juke box. The lounge is friendly and somewhat quieter with a tired 1950's decor. You will probably hear old soldiers discussing their war careers or what is going on at the British Legion. Paperbacks are sold in aid of the local fire brigade and there is a fruit machine.

There is a large car park at the front, a patio and garden to the rear with swings and covered alcoves with seating in case of poor weather. Popular entertainment on alternate Saturdays; either live music, karaoke or a beach party! Every other Sunday is quiz night.

The Holbury is open all day from 12 noon - 23.00, Monday to Saturday with normal Sunday hours. Dogs welcome but no children in the bars.

HUNTERS WINE BAR   58

24 The High Street, Lyndhurst. Tel (01703) 282217

Hunter's is not strictly a wine bar, it's a warm, local pub with marble topped tables and a popular restaurant. From the High Street the property looks a little swish but be assured that drinkers are very welcome and the bar is friendly. The building is 250 years old with a preservation order and smuggler's tunnels cross the road to the bank and to the church. There is a ghost that has been seen by some of the locals, she is quite friendly and does harmless things like putting the kettle on.

Hunter's is a free house serving Ringwood Best Bitter and Old Thumper on handpump, with Guinness, Red Stripe, Carlsberg and Heineken Export also on draught.

The food is good and not typically pub fayre. At lunchtime the emphasis is pies, game and poultry in season - such as roast duck and blackcurrant sauce £5.95. The evening menu changes all the time but one can expect dishes such as butterfly prawns deep-fried and served with a seasoned mayonnaise dip £3.95, escargot baked in garlic butter £2.95, fresh crab salad £3.60, roast pheasant served with an apricot and walnut stuffing £9.25, honey glazed lamb cutlets £8.95, salmon and prawn en croute served with crayfish sauce £8.95, gamekeeper's stew and crusty bread £6.50, medley of fresh fish grilled and served with a dill and parsley sauce £8.95 and whole fresh Dover sole grilled in lemon butter £10.95.

Hunters is open 11.00 - 15.00 and 18.00 - 23.00 and normal hours on Sundays. There is live music every Tuesday and Sunday, and taped music at other times. Check for special prices on beers. All credit cards except Diners and Amex accepted. Children and dogs at landlord's discretion.

INN ON THE FURLONG   59

Meeting House Lane, The Furlong, Ringwood. Tel (01425) 475139

A massive real fire welcomes you into this friendly, local bar. There is a stone floor, beams, and brick and panelled walls. Licencees, Andy and Deborah Morgan, have created "the sort of pub that they would like to walk into". The Inn on the Furlong is traditional in its attitudes as well as its food and beer. One of only two Ringwood Brewery pubs, the Furlong is noted for its hospitality. There are three cosy rooms off the main bar and nice touches such as newspapers, live music every Tuesday and special activities for the regulars. Before becoming a pub just ten years ago, the building was a wine and brandy merchants and still has the original cellars dating back to the beginning of the century.

Real ales include Ringwood Best, Old Thumper, Fortyniner, and Porter in the winter. A guest ale such as Thompson's Best Bitter is always on offer. John Smiths, Guinness, Batemans Champion Dark Mild, Fosters, Kronenbourg, Stonehouse cider and Merrydown are on draught.

If the bar is busy, which it frequently is, there is a restaurant for diners. Food is all homemade and the day's selection is printed on blackboards. All dishes are £3.95 or less, including the Sunday roast. Popular choices are leek and potato soup £1.50, local pork and leek sausages £2.00, seafood platter and chips £3.95, chilli-gone-barmy £2.50 and Stilton mushrooms £2.50.

The Inn on the Furlong is possibly the only pub in the country with 750 free car parking spaces and four bus stops adjacent, solving your parking and transport problems. There is a patio area both front and back. Dogs are welcome and there is a room for well behaved children.

The pub is currently open 11.00 - 15.00 and 17.00 - 23.00 Monday, Tuesday, and Thursday, and all day Wednesday, Friday, and Saturday. Normal Sunday hours.

INN AT THE PARK   60

Lyndhurst Park Hotel, Lyndhurst. Tel (01703) 283923

The Inn at the Park is a lively barn-like bar in the elegant Lyndhurst Park Hotel. Happy hours and live music every Tuesday contribute to its popularity with both hotel guests and locals.

Flowers Original, Ushers Best Bitter and Boddingtons are on handpump. Whitbread Best Bitter, Murphys stout, Heineken, Stella Artois and Scrumpy Jack cider are also on draught.

The snack menu is reasonably priced and includes garlic mushrooms £2.95, scampi and chips in the basket £4.50, prawn and mushroom tagliatelle £3.25, "Mr. Motivator" jacket potato £2.95, turkey and cranberry bumper bap £2.70 and New Forest sausages £3.50.

The pub is open 11.00 - 14.30 and 17.30 - 23.00 six days a week and normal Sunday hours. Children, dogs and credit cards welcome. Bed and breakfast £36.95 per person.

THE JOLLY SAILOR

Ashlet Creek, near Fawley. Tel (01703) 891305

You may have to ask the way as the Jolly Sailor is right at the end of the road just half-a-mile from Fawley village and signs are few and far between. It is an old pub, tastefully redecorated with wooden panels and plenty of cosy corners in the bar. There is a "Grockle tide guide" and shelf for magazines and local information. The restaurant area is fairly spacious and the walls are covered with photographs and prints of marine scenes. The outstanding view of the tiny Ashlet Creek, Southampton Water and Fawley village green is quite unspoilt despite its proximity to the refinery and the power station.

The pub boasts a ghost - what pub doesn't? - but more interestingly being situated at the water's edge, this is an old smuggler's pub and there is rumoured to be a tunnel coming out in the adjoining field.

The Jolly Sailor is a Whitbread pub partnership serving Flowers Original, Wadworth 6X, Morland Old Speckled Hen and a guest ale on handpump. Whitbread Best Bitter, Guinness, Murphys stout, Heineken, Stella Artois and Scrumpy Jack cider are also available on draught.

The food is medium priced but excellent value. You can choose anything from a sandwich to a T-bone steak, or one of the specials on the board. Most of the dishes are home-made, fresh fish is a speciality and the pub even smokes its own cheese. Choose from "Off Watch" snacks such as torpedo rolls from £1.95, half pint of prawns £5.35 and home-cooked ham ploughman's £3.25. 'Foredeck' starters include garlic mushrooms £2.75 and Ashlet smokie £3.25 while main courses range from fillet of plaice £4.95, moules mariniére £3.95 and £6.25, and chicken curry £5.50, to sole meuniére £8.75, sirloin steak £9.75 and seafood platter of tigertail prawns, prawns, giant greenlip mussels, cockles and whole dressed crab £12.50. Carefully selected wines from £6.95 a bottle.

Licensees, Tony and Sue Redfern, actively encourage 'boat people' who can moor in the creek or park on the quay. There are no pub gimmicks or outside facilities as such, just alfresco activities. Chilren are permitted in the pub if they are dining. Opening hours are 11.00 - 15.00 and 18.00 - 23.00 and the usual Sunday hours.

THE KINGS ARMS

St. Thomas Street, Lymington. Tel (01590) 672594

Situated at the top of the High Street, the Kings Arms is an unremarkable, half timbered pub dating back to Tudor times. The lounge bar is a dining room and the public bar, although "unspoilt" in character with kegs behind the bar, is only remarkable in that there is nothing on the walls. The regulars are however, some of the most memorable characters in the New Forest and you can be assured a warm welcome. Charles the Second is reputed to have stayed in the pub.

There is an excellent selection of real ales on sale. Four of the following real ales are always available; Marston's Pedigree, Gales HSB, Brakspear Bitter, Greene King Abbot Ale, Flowers Original, Pompey Royal, Winter Royal and Fullers Chiswick Bitter. Whitbread Best and Mild, Guinness, Heineken, Scrumpy Jack and Dry Blackthorn cider are also on draught.

Good homemade food. Soup £1.50, Hawaiian fruit cocktail £1.40, smoked mackerel with horseradish £1.70, Brie wedges deep fried £2.40, steak and kidney pie £3.95, chicken and ham pie £3.95, lasagne with garlic bread and salad £3.75, pork chop and apple sauce £4.75, grilled gammon and pineapple £6.95 and roast of the day £3.95. A specials board includes homemade lentil soup £1.50, roast lamb £3.95, meat or vegetable lasagne £3.75 and curry and rice £3.75. Vegetarian dishes also on a blackboard include cheese, onion and mushroom quiche £3.75. Sweets include strawberry sundae £1.95, coffee and butterscotch meringue £1.95 and cheese and biscuits £1.60.

Steve and Sandra Poingdestre pride themselves on not having a juke box, designer lagers, posing potions, a pool table, or piped music in the toilets. They do however offer bed and breakfast at £18.50 for a single room or £35 for a double or family room.

The Kings Arms is open 10.00 - 14.30 and 18.00 - 23.00 Monday to Friday. 10.00 - 17.00 and 18.00 - 23.00 Saturday. Normal Sunday hours. No children in the bars. Dogs welcome in the public bar. There is a carpark through a very narrow passage to the back where there is also limited outdoor seating.

KINGS HEAD INN   63

Quay Hill, Lymington. Tel (01590) 672709

Located at the top of the picturesque, cobbled Quay Hill, which is lined with 18th and 19th century bow windowed shops, the Kings Head has been a pub since 1836 and was originally the baker's shop. There are two bars with Tudor-style decor, open fireplaces, a collection of mugs and a comfortable window seat which affords a good view of the busy High Street.

Owned by Whitbread and run by Gary and Paul Stratton, this popular pub serves Whitbread Best Bitter, Boddingtons Bitter, Morland Old Speckled Hen, Guinness, Heineken, Stella Artois and Strongbow cider on draught. There is also an occasional guest ale and a seletion of well priced wines.

There is a large, varied and innovative menu at reasonable prices. You can choose from a simple cheese sandwich £1.75 to a King's grill with sirloin steak, sausage, gammon, lamb chop, venison and egg served with tomato, mushrooms and French fries £8.25. Other choices include Cajun prawn dippers £4.25, the Porker, a twelve inch sausage with French fries and relish £3.50, Paddy Magintys, special recipe sausages with mashed potato and Guinness and onion gravy £3.50, Baseys mussels, half a kilo of giant green lipped New Zealand mussels £6.25 and salmon fruits de mer £6.95. You can also create a number of your own dishes; jacket potatoes, omelettes and toasties come with your choice of two fillings. Kiddies dishes £1.95. You can order your favourite seafood by giving 24 hours notice. Food is served every day, Monday to Saturday from 11.00 till 22.00 and Sunday 12.00 to 14.30 and 19.00 till 21.30.

The pub is open from 11.00 - 23.00 Monday to Saturday and the normal Sunday hours. Children and dogs are welcome in the bars which are generally filled with a local crowd, visiting yachtsmen and tourists in the summer months because of its convenient and attractive location.

THE KINGS HEAD   64

Grove Lane, Redlynch, near Salisbury. Tel (01725) 510420

Peacefully located in the pretty Wiltshire village of Redlynch, just off the Cadnam to Downton road, the Kings Head is an attractive, old fashioned 400 year-old country pub. You will find a friendly, welcoming atmosphere, original low beams, log fires in winter, quiet background music and good "village prices". Ably run by Bernard Shorthouse, there is one main bar and an eating area where you can browse the Merchant Navy memorabilia! There are delightful country walks around the area and a spectacular bluebell wood in the spring.

This is an Ushers house dispensing Ushers Best Bitter, Strong Country Bitter, Courage Best and Directors on handpump, plus Whitbread Best Bitter, John Smiths Bitter, Guinness, Fosters, Kronenbourg and Scrumpy Jack cider.

Bar food is reasonably priced and includes lunchtime snacks and an evening menu in season. Items listed are sandwiches from £1.20, ploughman's £2.50, jumbo sausage, egg and chips £3, faggots with chips and peas £3.80, steak and kidney pie £4.50, chilli with rice or chips £3.50, fisherman's pie £3.50 or sirloin steak £7. For sweet, try perhaps the spotted dick, treacle pudding or apple or rhubarb crumble served with custard or cream £1.60. Winter roasts £5.50

Opening times are 12.00 - 14.30 and 18.00 - 23.00, Sunday hours are 19.00 - 22.30 only. Good large car park and pleasant garden for summer drinking. Families welcome as there is a separate children's room, and dogs are allowed inside. Bed and Breakfast accommodation with tea and coffee making facilities and TV, £15 per person.

THE LAMB INN   65

2 Hightown Road, Ringwood. Tel (01425) 473721

The Lamb Inn is a friendly village pub on the edge of the town and close to the old railway. The building is 250-years-old and has exposed beams, an artex ceiling, various brick work and comfortable wall seating. Numerous plates and old regional photographs line the walls and an inherited fish tank is a feature of the bar. This is a Whitbread property on lease to Greenall Whitney, and managed by Norman and Wendy Shepherd.

"This bar is dedicated to those who make drinking a pleasure, who reach contentment before capacity, and who can take it, hold it, and still remain gentlemen".

Whitbread Best Bitter, Guinness, Heineken, Stella Artois and Dry Blackthorn cider are served on draught. Royal Wessex Bitter is the only real ale available.

This is not really a food pub, but reasonably priced pub fayre is available, including a full English breakfast £3.50. Bar food includes prawn cocktail £2, sandwiches and rolls from £1.30, baked potatoes with side salad from £1.80, ham or beef ploughman's £3.25, chicken, chips and peas £3.75, cheeseburger £2.75, chicken nuggets £2.75, plaice and chips £3.75 and steak £6.95. Sweets £2 include apple pie and cream, treacle sponge and custard, and spotted dick and custard. A pot of tea and toasted teacake £1.50 for two can also be ordered.

The pub offers darts, dominoes, pool, bar billiards, Sky TV, disabled access, a walled patio garden and a kids room with games. Well mannered dogs and similarly behaved children are allowed in the bar.

The Lamb Inn is open 11.00 - 15.00 and 18.00 - 23.00 and normal Sunday hours. Three bedrooms, popular with fishermen, are available for bed and breakfast at £35 a double and early breakfasts and flasks will be provided if required.

Burley Road, Winkton. Tel (01425) 672427

The Lamb Inn is a country pub built in the 1700's and used as a smugglers inn. There is a creditable selection of real ales, informal Victorian decor and a friendly atmosphere with a good local trade. The two bars, lounge and public, are spacious with beams and adorned with country bits and pieces.

The Lamb is a free house and at the time of visiting Isle of Wight Nipper, Daleside Bitter, Monkey Wrench, Greene King Abbot Ale, Fullers London Pride, Bass, Ringwood Best Bitter and Ringwood Old Thumper were on handpump. Worthington Bitter, M & B Mild, McEwan's Export, Lowenbrau and Carling Black Label were also available on draught.

As well as the two bars there is a restaurant and conservatory area for diners. The food is good value. The bar menu includes sandwiches from £1.30, open sandwiches such as Caribbean prawn salad and seafood dressing topped with caviar for £2.95, ploughman's from £2.50, eggs harlequin £2.50, filled jacket potatoes from £2.50, salads from £3.95, homemade steak and kidney pie £4.75, chicken curry £3.75, mixed grill £6.50, chicken Kiev £4.95, jumbo cod in batter £4.75, sausage and chips in a basket £2.25 and mushroom stroganoff £5.95. The specials board features home-cooked favourites such as smothered steak £6.95. Children's dishes from £1.50. Desserts include grandma's toffee sponge with fudge sauce, toffee and pecan pie, lemon lush and various cheesecakes all £2.25.

The Lamb is open 11.00 - 14.30 and 17.00 - 23.00 Monday to Friday, all day Saturday and Bank Holidays and normal Sunday opening. There is a beer garden with children's play area and facilities inside include a pool table, darts, shove halfpenny and piped music. Live country and western music is popular on Sunday nights, as are the winter quiz nights. Dogs are allowed in the public bar and garden. Children welcome inside.

Forest Edge Road, Nomansland, Salisbury, Wiltshire. Tel (01794) 390246

This idyllically situated pub lies on the Wiltshire/Hampshire border so that one can sit in the Wiltshire bar and watch a game of cricket outside in Hampshire. Many years ago customers would move bars at closing since one county closed earlier than the other! The interior is "Foresty" in decor with exposed beams, open fires, antlers, barrel seats and an unusual thatched bar. It is a pub for all ages, and busy with both tourists and locals.

Run by Ray and Iris Langridge, the Lamb is a Whitbread property serving real ales - Flowers Original Bitter and Wadworth 6X - Whitbread Best Bitter, Boddingtons Mild, Guinness, Murphys stout, Heineken, Stella Artois and Strongbow cider on draught.

Food prices are extremely reasonable for the substantial dishes on offer. Menu choices include, freshly made sandwiches from £1.45, deep fried mushrooms with garlic or blue cheese dip £1.85, whitebait £1.60, honey roast ham ploughman's £2.75, quarter-pound beefburger with fries £2.25, bacon, egg and chips £1.90, prawn and tuna salad £3.95, lasagne and salad £4.25, cottage pie with crusty bread £2.75, steak'n ale pie £4.50, crispy cod coated in natural breadcrumbs served with lemon and tartare sauce £3.75, mixed grill with almost everything £6.95 and an 8oz sirloin steak £6.75. The vegetarian blackboard lists spinach and ricotta cheese cannelloni, Stilton and leek bake and vegetable tikka masala with rice, all £4.50. Apple, cherry or apricot pie, sticky toffee pudding, apple fudge cake and treacle pudding from £1.25 feature on the pudding board. Sunday roasts.

The pub opens 11.00 - 23.00 (according to demand), all day Saturday and normal Sunday hours. Activities include darts, pool and live entertainment once a month. Roadside tables, chairs and brollies - a garden is planned - and dogs welcome inside.

LANDFORD POACHER 68

Pound Hill, Landford, near Romsey. Tel (01794) 390353

The Landford Poacher is a well run country pub catering for all the family. It is tastefully decorated and successfully combines a lively bar area with a discrete restaurant. The beamed bar is adorned with guns, stuffed birds and pewter mugs and boasts the most comfortable bar stools in the area. Manageress, Sue Cutler, ensures that there is always something going on and plenty of special offers on food and drink. At Christmas time the pub displays some of the best festive decorations to be found in the Forest.

As a free house there is a good selection of beers and lagers with Webster's Yorkshire Bitter, Beamish, Mild, Fosters and Carlsberg Export available on draught. Cask conditioned real ales served on handpump are Ruddles Best Bitter, Courage Directors and Ruddles County.

The Poacher presents good value home-cooked food from a lunch and bar menu, and from the imaginative a la carte menu, which includes such delicacies as frogs legs. The bar menu offers the standard favourites, such as steak sandwich, lasagne, chilli con carne and curry, all £3.50, sandwiches £1.60 and stuffed jacket potatoes £2.10. Children's menu at £2.25.

Opening hours are 11.30 - 15.00 and 18.30 - 23.00 Monday to Saturday with a midnight license for diners. Usual Sunday hours. Coaches welcome.

Facilities include a pool table, pin ball machine and a garden, and for children a pets corner complete with aviary, the Landford witch and Hector the 18-stone pot-bellied pig. In the old days lorry drivers used to stop overnight in the garden sheds but today the Poacher offers bed and breakfast in a self-catering chalet. Prices range from £15 for single occupancy to £35 for a family of six.

LANGLEY TAVERN 69

Lepe Road, Langley, near Blackfield. Tel (01703) 891402

This is a pleasantly decorated, pre-war, village pub, very friendly and popular with both locals and tourists on the Exbury and Lepe routes. There are two bars; the spacious public, appealing to the locals, is smart by average standards, fully carpeted and comfortably decorated in green and cream, and the lounge, freshly redecorated with tables for diners, comfortable window seating and a conservatory where parents can watch their children play in the huge beer garden with every sort of entertainment for offspring, including three trampolines, climbing frame, bouncy castle, swing boats and Wendy house.

This is a Whitbread pub leased to the welcoming hosts Sue and Trevor Emery. Real ales include Wadworth 6X and Boddingtons Bitter on handpump, with Whitbread Best Bitter, Guinness, Mild, Heineken, Heineken Export, Stella Artois and Strongbow cider also on draught.

Very reasonably priced food starts at £1 for sandwiches, light bites such as pâté with hot toast and salad garnish for £1.45, jumbo jackets from £1.75, ploughman's from £2.75, American burger with salad and a sesame bun with chips £2.10, prime sirloin steak cooked to your liking with salad garnish, chips and peas, or jacket potato £5.95, lasagne with salad £2.95, steak and kidney pie with peas and a choice of potato £3.75, vegetarian dish of the day and sweets from £1.45.

The Langley Tavern offers excellent value, en-suite bed and breakfast for £15 per person. Every room has colour TV, and tea and coffee making facilities.

The pub is open all day, 11.00 - 23.00, with normal Sunday hours. Adult facilities include darts, pool, fruit machines, Sky TV and petanque.

Station Road, Fordingbridge. Tel (01425) 652098

Located just one mile from Fordingbridge on the Damerham road, the Load of Hay is a local's pub which could not, by any stretch of the imagination, be called artificial. Built pre-turn of the century, this old coaching stop changed its name from The Railway Hotel in 1966 and has a simply decorated lounge bar, public bar, function room and its original cellars.

Owned by Eldridge Pope and run by licencees Nick and Chris Bartley, one will find their Royal Oak, Dorchester Bitter and Hardy Country Ale on handpump plus EP Best Bitter, Tetley Bitter, Guinness, Carlsberg, Carlsberg Export and Dry Blackthorn cider on draught.

There is a separate lunch and evening menu, the latter specialising in fish, poultry and steaks. A regularly changing specials board features dishes like deep pan pizza, chips and salad £2.95, chicken Kiev £3.50, peppered mackerel £2.95, lemon sole £3.95 and mixed grill £4.50. The typical pub lunch dishes include beefburger £1.30 and sausage, egg and chips £2.10, ploughman's £2.75, homemade cottage pie and battered cod fillet both £3. On the pudding list are treacle sponge £1.50 and hot chocolate fudge cake with cream £1.55.

The Load of Hay is open 11.00 - 15.00 and 18.00 - 23.00 weekdays, all day Saturday and normal Sunday hours. As well as fruit- and quiz- machines and a juke box there are plenty of local activities arranged around the pub, such as folk and country and western music and clay pigeon shooting. Annual pumpkin and giant vegetable competition on the last Saturday in September. Small garden area with tables and barbecue. Dogs and children welcome. Overnight accommodation in six bedrooms with tea and coffee making facilities and TV £15 per person.

THE LORD NELSON 71

High Street, Hythe. Tel (01703) 842169

Situated next to the Hythe Ferry, the Lord Nelson is 465 years old and still maintains a lot of its original charm, including outside loos. Originally a customs house, the building became a pub in 1801. Lord Nelson is said not only to have stayed in the pub but also to have met Lady Hamilton there, and his ghost is supposed to haunt the pub. There are three enchanting, unspoilt and extremely small bars, the Poop Deck, Trafalgar and Victory, all wood panelled with low beams. The clientele includes a strong Irish contingent as well as genuine locals. Being very close to Southampton Water, a number of the more 'mature' locals will recall standing at the bar in wellies at high tide! Indeed the view over the water is exhilarating.

This is a Whitbread property run by Adam and Rona Mosley, with five real ales - Strong Country Bitter, Flowers Original, Wadworth 6X, Ringwood Porter and Ringwood Best Bitter on handpump. Whitbread Best Bitter, Mild, Guinness, Heineken, Stella Artois, Bulmers Traditional and Inches Stonehouse cider are also on draught.

The Lord Nelson has one of the cheapest menus in the Forest; filled baguettes from £2.25, fried egg sandwich £1.35, a simple steak and kidney pie £1.75, a more substantial fish platter £4.10, omelette with any combination of cheese, honey roast ham, mushroom, tomato or onion £2.95, bumper all day breakfast £3.45 and chicken, ham and leek pie £1.75.

Open all day - 11.00 - 23.00 weekdays and normal Sunday hours. Dogs and children welcome and there is a garden area overlooking the water.

Linford Road, Poulner, near Ringwood. Tel (01425) 473819

You could not drive past this unpretentious, village pub during the summer months, without being dazzled by the spectacular pots and hanging baskets. The Tavern is a warm, local pub which hosts, Odge Hodkinson and Eric Richards, claim "is not the trendiest, but is the friendliest" - even the customer's dogs receive at least one biscuit. There is just one traditional, panelled bar with a hatch through to the garden where there is a chalet for children. A further family room is planned. The bar has comfortable window seats, nautical brass nick-nacks, ceiling fans, a collection of zippo lighters and heated by a warm log fire in the winter. The buidling, part of which was shops, is 200-300 years old, on the old London Road. Linford Bottom, a popular picnic spot and paddling stream on the edge of the Forest, is close by, as is the 19th century, picturesque, mud and thatch, Poulner Baptist Church.

The Tavern is on a Whitbread lease dispensing well kept real ales such as Fuller's Chiswick Bitter, Greene King Abbot Ale, Castle Eden Bitter and Ringwood Best Bitter. Whitbread Best Bitter, Guinness, Heineken, Stella Artois and Stonehouse cider are also on draught.

The menu may change once the new landlords have settled in but will consist of cheap, traditional pub food. This includes sandwiches from £1.15, smoked ham toastie £1.50, Cornish pasties £1.50, ploughman's £2.50, a hot sausage buttie with two bangers £1.25, Melton Mowbray pork pie 95p and homemade chilli with French bread £2.75. No sweets currently.

There are summer Saturday bring-your-own barbecues, occasional live entertainment, darts, dominoes and Purbeck stone shove halfpenny on a long board.

The Tavern is open 11.00 - 15.00 and 18.00 - 23.00 weekdays and normal Sunday hours. Extended summer opening on Friday and Saturday. There is a large car park at the rear through a narrow wall entrance.

High Street, Lyndhust. Tel (01703) 284196

Driving through Lyndhust, you could miss the Mailman's so you would be well advised to leave your car in the main "free" car park adjacent to the New Forest Museum and walk the few hundred yards to the junction of the Southampton and Brockenhurst roads. The Mailman's, the only pub in Britain with this name, is located at the back of the garage forecourt. This is a friendly, unpretentious pub despite boasting an entry in the Good Beer Guide and awards for its cooking and its garden. Originally a coaching inn, the decor is currently basic and generally appeals to a middle-age group.

The pub first gained a reputation for its well kept real ales when a previous landlord, Larry Walder gained television fame for talking to the beers to bring them to their peak. Current licensees, Alistair Gray and Julie Duffet will not be talking to the beers but they do aim to serve them in top condition. Mailman's is a Marston pub offering Marston's Best Bitter and Pedigree on handpump plus John Smiths Bitter, Guinness, Heineken, Becks, Stella Artois and Strongbow cider on draught.

The pub is known for its good, home-cooked food. The new menu will specialise in fresh local fish and seafood with a daily specials board and a selection of homemade sweets. Prices will start at £2.25 for half a pint of prawns, mussels £3.75, scallops £4.50, king prawns and scallops cooked in garlic, ginger, black bean and wine £6.95 and whole baked crab from £10. A new restaurant area is planned at the rear as part of a complete refit in February following a Forest theme. Summer Spanish and Portuguese style barbecues are planned in the garden with live folk music.

Another distinguishing feature of the Mailman's is that there is no juke box, no video, no fruit machines and no dogs. There is however background music. The pub is open 11.00 - 15.00 and 18.00 - 23.00 Monday to Saturday and normal Sunday hours. After Easter the pub plans to open all day.

The Master Builders House Hotel, Bucklers Hard, Beaulieu. Tel (01590) 616253

Located within the Master Builders House Hotel, the Yachtsman's bar opens onto the historic and picturesque Buckler's Hard and for that reason should not be missed. The nearby Maritime museum records the shipbuilding history of the village where Nelson's fleet was built and recreates 18th century life with a shipwright's cottage and a labourer's abode. The bar formed part of the original village famous for building ships since 1698 and smuggler's tunnels lead from the pub. The comfortable, stone floored bar is rectangular with a separate area for diners and features photographs of yachts and ships as well as original beams, lanterns and a substantial open fireplace. The clientele is a mixture of hotel guests, tourists and locals using the marina.

The pub offers Allied Brewery ales - Tetley Bitter and Ind Coope Burton Ale - on handpump with John Bull Bitter, Guinness, Lowenbrau, Castlemaine 4X and Strongbow cider also on draught.

A food counter offers sandwiches from £1.75, salads £3.95, soup of the day £1, filled jacket potato £2, ploughman's £3.50, beef curry with rice £3.95 and dishes of the day £4.95, such as chicken and vegetable stew, lemon sole, chilli con carne and guinea fowl. Sunday roast from £4.95. Standard gâteaux and fruit pies for dessert £1.95. Afternoon teas £1.

The pub is open 11.00 - 15.00 and 18.30 - 23.00, all day Saturday and normal Sunday hours. Well appointed overnight accommodation with en-suite facilities and four posters (from £55 single, £85 double). Children are welcome, and dogs, except in the buffet area. Secluded beer garden and patio area as well as outside seating in the village during the summer.

Bramble Hill Hotel, Bramshaw, near Lyndhurst. Tel (01703) 813165

The Gallery bar is an elegant, comfortable bar located within the Bramble Hill Hotel, which was once a Medieval hunting lodge. Delightfully situated in well maintained gardens in arguably one of the most beautiful settings in the New Forest, the hotel is private and secluded, although it is just two miles from the M27. The ambience of the Gallery bar is far more sophisticated than the average pub, with high ceilings, wood panelled walls, stags heads, hunting horns and a 17th century brick and flint fireplace contributing to the atmosphere - pity about the pictures! Behind the bar elaborately carved oak shelving houses drinks and glasses.

This free house offers four changing real ales - Ringwood Porter (winter), Old Thumper, Old Bramble (Fortyniner), Bass and London Pride. Worthington Best Bitter, Guinness, Fosters, Carling Black Label, Tennent's Extra and Scrumpy Jack cider are also on draught. Interesting wine list.

There is a restaurant offering fish game and steaks, but the bar menu offers a varied selection of seasonal fayre. The choices include sandwiches from £2.25, brunch, up to midday, of either full English breakfast £5 or corned beef hash with eggs £3.50, prawn cocktail £2.95, garlic mushrooms £2.45, scampi and chips £5.45, rump steak £6.50, pie of the day £5.25 and lasagne £4.95. Daily changing blackboard specials may feature tandoori chicken £5.25, homemade venison pie £6.50 and grilled trout £5.25. Sweets £2.25 include New Forest bramble pie, strawberry tarts and chocolate fudge gateau. Cream tea £3.

Summer activities range from barbecues, banquets and live music to tea dances. Marquee for functions.

Dogs on leads are welcomed and children can eat in the Garden bar dining area. Alternatively there is plenty of open space and woodland walks outside for fine weather days. Overnight accommodation in ten en-suite rooms from £30 double (£100 for family suite) Open all day 11.00 - 23.00. Credit cards are accepted.

Editor's note
At the time of going to press we learnt that the name Mops had been dropped and that in future the bar would simply be known as the Bramble Hill Hotel.

THE MORANT ARMS   76

Brookley Road, Brockenhurst. Tel (01590) 23333

The Morant Arms is a quiet, traditional, local pub managed by Peter and Thelma Taylor. The name comes from the Morant family who owned half of Brockenhurst in the pre-war period. The pretty, pine panelled lounge bar is circular in design and handy for the railway station. The public sports bar is more tastefully decorated than most and has a sunken pool playing area. There is also a family room upstairs, away from the bars, that also caters for small functions.

Real ales available are, Dorchester Bitter, Hardy Country Ale and Royal Oak. Eldridge Pope Best Biter, Guinness, Labatt's, Carlsberg Export and Taunton Dry Blackthorn cider are also served on draught.

The food is cheap and tasty, current prices starting at £1.75 for sandwiches and £1.90 for toastie and salad. Other snacks include pâté of the day £2.95, jacket potato with prawns £2.25, beefburger in a sesame bun £1.95, bacon in a hot crusty French stick £2.50 and home-cooked ham ploughman's £3.00. More substantial dishes featured are breaded plaice fillet and tartar sauce £4.25, ham, egg and chips £3.75, fluffy 3-egg omelettes £3.45, rump steak £6.25 and mixed grill with chips and all the trimmings £6.25. Traditional Sunday roast £4.95 and for puddings, apple pie, cheesecake, crumbles and gâteaux £1.95. Standard children's menu £2.25.

The Morant Arms is conveniently located next to a craft shop and bike-hire, ironic since a notice over the public bar reads "no bikers"! Children are welcome away from the bar and dogs when and where, food is not being served. There is a fenced garden with swings, trampoline and climbing frame and the pub offers bed and breakfast accommodation - not en-suite - at £15 per person, (£17.50 in the peak season between Spring and August Bank Holiday). A full English breakfast is included and packed lunches can be arranged.

Opening hours are 11.00 - 15.00 and 18.00 - 23.00 weekdays and normal Sunday hours.

MORTIMERS TAVERN   77

Romsey Road, Ower. Tel (01703) 814379

Mortimers is conveniently situated at the entrance to Paultons Park just off junction 2 of the M27. The building was probably the dower house for the original estate and is now managed by Anne and Pete Gay. There are two square, traditionally decorated bars and a comfortable restaurant area. The pub is probably best described as a family pub with a neat garden, an enclosed children's garden with swings, see-saw and climbing frame, plus a functions room and a skittle alley.

As a free house, there is a varied selection of real ales on offer, including Ringwood Best Bitter and Ansells Original. Also on draught are Whitbread Best Bitter, Guinness, Mild, Castlemaine 4X, Heineken, Stella Artois and Strongbow cider.

On the food side there is a long specials board and a menu offering snacks and sandwiches from £1.25 or, alternatively, a full meal. Starters may include egg and prawn mayonnaise £2.95, smoked salmon £3.75, whitebait £2.95 and breaded mushrooms £2.85. More substantial dishes range from chilli and rice £3.95, lasagne and chips £4.60, savoury Lincolnshire sausages £4.20 and roast beef and Yorkshire pudding £4.60 to garlic French stick with cheese and prawns £2.95 and fillet steak stroganoff £4.75. Sweets £1.75 include passion cake, apple pie and custard, funky monkey peanut pie and ginger pudding and custard. Reasonable wine list including house selections at £5.95.

Nearby is Paulton's, a family leisure park set in 140 acres with Capability Brown gardens, a lake, over 1,000 exotic birds in well placed avaries, magic forest, minature railway, bumper boats, village life museum and llamas, deer, capybaras and farm animals.

Mortimers is the perfect respite from the pleasure park, and is open from 11.00 - 15.00 and 17.30 - 23.00 and normal Sunday hours. Visa. Dogs are not allowed in the bar. B&B accommodation is offered with tea and coffee making facilities, (£25 single and £40 double).

MUSKETEER 78

North Street, Pennington, near Lymington. Tel (01590) 676527

Built around 1910 this unspoilt, one bar village pub does not welcome change and displays a charming lack of attempt to make it twee; its simple but clean. The history is a little vague but originally named the Lion and Lamb, and sold as a free house 18 years ago, the Musketeer evolved. Run by licensees, Phil and Eve, the bar is frequented by dedicated locals with tweed suits and cloth caps. You could be forgiven for thinking it a male bastion but have no fears, this very special pub welcomes women! The decor is basic with settles, yellowed artex walls and a sturdy wooden bar with foot rail. The only thing that surprised us was the absense of a spittoon! Perhaps the only criticism we had was the apparent and inappropriate, Nordic replica weaponry; an engagingly naive attempt to decorate the walls with the sort of stuff that people have come to expect.

You will be pleased not to be greeted by the smell of chips. Simple wholesome food is served. Sandwiches, ploughman's and homemade soups at very reasonable prices. The Musketeer, featured in CAMRA'S Good Beer Guide, dispenses real ales, Ringwood Best Bitter, Brakspear Bitter, Gales HSB, Draught Bass, Smiles Exhibition and guest beers such as Greene King Abbot Ale, Adnams Southwold Bitter and Shepherd Neame Best Bitter on handpump. Worthington Best Bitter, Guinness, Tennent's Pilsner, Tennent's Extra and Copperhead cider are also on draught.

Dogs are permitted but no music, machines or children. Opening hours are 12.00 - 15.00 Monday to Friday (11.30 - 15.00 Saturday) 17.30 - 23.00 and normal Sunday hours. If you like "real" pubs do not miss the Musketeer.

THE NAGS HEAD 79

Moortown, near Ringwood. Tel (01425) 473263

The original Nags Head is the little cottage next door. The current building was purpose built in 1938. The pub forms the centre of the local community attracting both local trade and the passer-by on the busy Christchurch road.

This is an Eldridge Pope property serving Dorchester Bitter, Hardy Country and Royal Oak on handpump. EP Best, Guinness, Carlsberg, Carlsberg Export and Dry Blackthorn cider are also on draught.

Landlords Michael and Gillian Carter present traditional pub fayre including prawn cocktail £2.30, cod in batter £3.95, stir fried vegetables in Szechuan sauce £4.25, chicken Madras curry £4.50 and 16oz. rump steak £8.95. There is a separate kids menu £2.25, specials board, sweets from £1.50 and Sunday roast £4.95. House wine £5.95.

The Nags Head is open 11.00 - 15.00 and 17.00 - 23.00 six days a week and normal Sunday hours. Dogs and children welcome. Children's play area and large garden.

THE NEW FOREST HOTEL   80

Lyndhurst Road, Ashurst. Tel (01703) 292319

The New Forest Hotel bar describes itself as a family tavern with a spacious
restaurant overlooking the Forest. The plushly furnished, L-shaped bar is devoid
of any clear theme but much of the huge bar is filled with table football, pool table
and juke box, and is particularly lively in the evenings attracting a youthful
clientele from nearby Totton. Local bands play most Fridays and Saturdays, and
there is a skittles room and a large garden with play equipment.

The pub is a free house run by Stewart Thornley and at the time of visiting
offered Friary Meux Best Bitter, Ind Coope Burton Ale and Tetley Bitter on
handpump, with Ansells Bitter, Guinness, Mild, Castlemaine 4X, Labatt's, Lowenbrau and Copperhead cider also served on draught.

There is an innovative bar snack menu, a restaurant menu and a carvery.
Dishes include Smokey Joes chilli flavoured chicken wings £2.00, chicken saté £2,
crispy mushrooms £2.25, filled jacket potatoes from £2.50, sandwiches from £1.50,
garlic chicken £7.25, trout £7.25, make your own salads with Norwegian prawns
or Dorset ham £6.95, pizzas from £4.50 to eat in or takeaway, and hot roast joint of
the day £7.99. Child sized carvery is £3.95. Sweets from the servery include treacle
tart, banoffee pie, lemon meringue pie, coffee and walnut gâteau and strawberry
shortbread, all £2.50.

The opening hours are currently 11.00 - 14.30 and 17.00 - 23.00 weekdays,
Sunday, 12.00 - 14.30 and normal evening hours. Limited Bed and Breakfast
accommodation £40 double.

NEW FOREST INN   81

Emery Down, Lyndhurst. Tel (01703) 282329   * "Good Food" award

The New Forest Inn is delightfully set in woodland on the edge of this pretty
hamlet and is a popular destination for Forest visitors and for the New Forest
ponies which congregate by the door, enhancing the pub's charm. The land,
claimed from the King by squatters in the 1700's, became the site of a caravan
trader selling groceries and ale. This caravan now forms the front lounge
porchway and part of the bar. Behind lies a bustling, well furnished, open-plan
bar with comfortable alcoves, and decorated with country bric-a-brac.

The pub is owned by Whitbread and newly managed by Mike Grove. Real ales
on handpump include Whitbread Strong Country, Wadworth 6X and Gales HSB
with Whitbread Best Bitter, Guinness, Murphys stout, Heineken and Stella
Artois also available on draught. Gales Country wines £1.60 per glass.

Noted for its reliable, home-cooked food the main menu includes fresh crab pâté
£3.50, mussels in cracked pepper sauce £3.50, pear Geneva on toast with
cranberries and hot Stilton sauce with salad £4.25, Cumberland sausages with
chips and onion gravy £4.25, fillet of salmon in champagne sauce £8.25, escallop of
veal cooked in sherry and cream £8.25 and fillet steak served with salad and
French fries £10.25. The specials board advertises a number of game dishes in
season, for example pheasant in port and redcurrant £7.50. Sweets £2.75 may
include toasted lemon bruleé and spotted dick. Wine by the bottle from £8.25.

The bar is open all day from 11.00 - 23.00 and normal Sunday hours. Excellent
alfresco drinking can be engaged in the splendid three-level garden which is full
of flower borders and mature shrubs. Comfortable overnight accommodation in
four en-suite bedrooms. Dogs and children are welcome inside. Credit cards
accepted. The New Forest Inn features in Egon Ronay's 'Pubs and Inns' and is
recommended by Les Routiers.

Avon, near Christchurch. Tel (01425) 672432

Built around 1830 and named after the then new Queen Victoria, this is a family orientated pub with a spacious but still comfortable lounge, cosy public bar, attractive covered patio, well kept beer garden stretching down to the river and a good size play area for children. The pub has been lovingly decorated with real fires in both bars and nice touches such as free matches. The bar too has been cleverly designed to allow you to see through from the public to the lounge area.

The New Queen is a Badger property serving Badger Best Bitter, Tanglefoot Double Gold and Ringwood Best Bitter on handpump. BXB Bitter, Guinness, Worthington Dark Mild, Muchener Pilsner, Royal Hofbrau and Hofbrau Export lager are also on draught.

Landlord, Alasdair Gilmore emphasises that the food is home-cooked along traditional lines. Starters all priced around £2 include whitebait and coronation chicken. Homemade house specialities include steak and kidney pie £4.25 and home-baked ham £3.75. Dishes for the smaller appetite are all priced at £2.25 and include mini ploughman's. Sandwiches start at £1.55. Sweets include black cherry surprise £2.45. House wine £5.99.

The New Queen is open 11.30 - 14.30 and 18.00 - 23.00 six days a week with normal Sunday hours. There is an interesting walk around the area with a map available at the bar. Walkers are welcome in the public bar. Popular music quiz night every Thursday. Dogs, children, horses, Access and Visa welcome.

Pinkney Lane, Bank, Lyndhurst. Tel (01703) 282350

Originally called the "Royal Oak", - it once had a tunnel from Queens House in Lyndhurst to the inn to allow the royals to escape in the event of trouble. Today the Oak Inn is a delightful old Forest pub with records dating back to 1719, and is in an idyllic setting surrounded by majestic oaks. This small pub has been recently restored with old, if not original, wooden floors and panelling and a tasteful mixture of new and old furnishings. The tiles from the fireplace, decorated with Shakespearian scenes, came from the house where Alice Liddle, the inspiration for Alice in Wonderland, lived.

This is a free house owned by Nick and Sue Wateridge. Real ales drawn straight from the cask include Hall and Woodhouse Tanglefoot, Whitbread Castle Eden Ale, Ringwood Best Bitter, Ringwood Fortyniner, Old Thumper and Courage Directors. Whitbread Best Bitter, Whitbread Mild, Murphys, Guinness, Heineken, Heineken Export, Stella Artois, Bulmers Original cider and Scrumpy Jack are also on draught.

The menu includes Forester's lunch from £2.80, a large bowl of delicious homemade soup £2, oak logs from £1.80, King prawns cooked in garlic butter £5.95, jumbo battered cod £4.95, Cajun prawns £4.95, ham, egg and chips £3.95, chicken breast £5.75 and 8oz sirloin steak £8.25. Specials are posted on blackboards with an average price of £4 and may include spicy chicken wings and salad £4.25, beef and pepper casserole served with a hunk of crusty bread £4.45, poached salmon salad £4.95, double lamb chop £3.95 or venison sausage with Cumberland sauce £3.25. Ploughman's come with five different pickles and the thick, oak wedge sandwiches are a filling snack.

The Oak Inn is open from 11.00 - 14.30 and 18.00 - 23.00 weekdays and normal Sunday hours. The ladies loo is smart with marble topped basin and pine panels. Dogs are permitted and children away from the bar. There is a fenced, shady garden with chipmunks and pigmy goats, but limited parking.

Ibsley, near Ringwood. Tel (01425) 473387

Originally three 14th century worker's cottages located on the Somerley estate, the Old Beams is a very pretty, and very popular, thatched free house, owned by Douglas and Jenny Major. Situated on the main Ringwood to Fordingbridge road, the pub attracts a lot of day trippers at lunch-time. Inside, the large open-plan bar has rough cast, plastered walls, heavy, centuries-old oak beams and a collection of sturdy wooden tables and chairs. There is also a tiny snug, a comfortable conservatory, garden, plus a canopied outside seating area.

The list of real ales is impressive: Gibbs Mew Bishop's Tipple, Ringwood Old Thumper and Best Bitter, Eldridge Pope Royal Oak, Wadworth 6X and Gales HSB. Also on draught are John Bull Bitter, Tetley Bitter, Double Diamond Export Ale, Guinness, Ind Coope Dark Mild, Skol Lager, Castlemaine 4X, Carlsberg Export, Lowenbrau, Swan Light Low Alcohol, Olde English and Addlestones cider.

There is a pretty restaurant with its own menu but the bar has a popular servery with the day's dishes listed on blackboards behind. Service is efficient although the tanoy system can be a little obtrusive. The salad bar is attractive with cold meat plates £5.90, with prawn or crab £6.70. Other choices include hot meat rolls £2.45, roast of the day £6.30, homemade steak and kidney pie £5.70 and curried beef or turkey £4.40. The á la carte board highlights gammon steak, duck a l'orange, braised oxtail and pork chop in cider. Prices range from £3.25 for shepherds pie to £10.65 for Dover sole. The sweet bar could match any in London and includes homemade specialities, chocolate fudge gâteau, fruit pies, trifles, chocolate mousse and lemon meringue pie, all around £2.25.

The Old Beams is open from 10.30 - 14.30 and 18.00 to 23.00 Monday to Saturday and the usual hours on Sunday. Children are very welcome in the main eating area and restaurant, but dogs are not allowed in. Credit cards accepted.

Lime Kiln Lane, Holbury. Tel (01703) 891137

You won't be disappointed when you find this 'olde worlde', thatched pub. The Old Mill Inn was originally a miller's cottage, parts of the pub dating back to the 12th century. This is a comfortable ale house with two bars, dried hops hanging from the ceiling, a real fire and plenty of nooks and crannies for discreet pleasure. It is one of those pubs where everything appears to run smoothly, presumably, something to do with the manageress, Elaine Ashby. There is a large restaurant that can be hired for private functions, and a games room with pool and darts.

There are usually nine real ales such as Felinfoel Double Dragon, Old Thumper, Old Mill, Ringwood Fortyniner, Porter, Tanglefoot, Courage Best, Websters Bitter and Courage Director's. Also on draught John Smiths, Guinness, Beamish, Carlsberg Export, Kronenbourg, Fosters, Kaliber, Scrumpy Jack cider and Red Rock.

The emphasis is on family eating although this is also a popular venue for businessmen. Dishes include pâté with hot toast £1.65, potato skins fom £1.95, cold tiger prawns on a bed of ice £2.15, butterfly prawns with tartare sauce £2.15. Fish dishes include fillet of plaice filled with prawns and mushrooms £4.95 and grilled salmon steak and hot butter sauce, £6.45. Whole roast chicken £4.25, Barbery duck and orange sauce £5.95, a substantial mixed grill £7.75, surf and turf £7.50 and an 8oz. rump for a mere £4.45. Sunday roast £4.95. Sweets from £1.95. House wine £6.95.

The Old Mill hosts live entertainment every Tuesday and every other Sunday. There is a children's play area, fish pond and garden. The large car park overlooks Dark Water Spring. Dogs are permitted in the bars. All major credit cards, except Diners, are accepted. The pub is open 11.00 - 15.00 and 17.00 - 23.00 during the week and all day Saturday. Normal Sunday hours.

Market Place, Ringwood. Tel (01425) 472702

The White Hart sign is seen on pubs all over the country. This name is believed to date back to the 15th century in the reign of Henry VII. The King took Archduke Philip of Spain and his wife Joan into the New Forest, hunting. They pursued a magnificent stag called Albert who gave a gallant run before being brought to bay. Joan was so impressed with his courage that she insisted his life be spared. It is recorded that the hunting party repaired to the local inn at Ringwood and, to commemorate Albert, the inn was renamed the White Hart.

Originally a coaching inn the White Hart has all the space of a hotel but the character of a friendly local pub. There are three large, panelled bars, with huge beams, open log fires, a splendid glass serving hatch and a relaxed atmosphere. Landlord Fred Walker boasts 21 years experience.

This is an Eldridge Pope tenancy offering Carlsberg, Carlsberg Export, Castlemaine 4X, Kronenbourg, Labatt's, Guinness and Dry Blackthorn cider on draught. Real Ales include Eldridge Pope Best, Hardy Country and Royal Oak.

There is a specials board changing daily, lite bites, Sunday roasts and dishes for the really hungry. These are all reasonably priced and include a steak baton for £2.95, wings of fire-marinated chicken wings £2.45, peppered mackerel £2.45, jumbo sausage in French bread £1.40, homemade cottage pie £3.25, crispy coated vegetables with dip £2.25, half rack of pork rib in BBQ sauce £4.95, homemade quiche £3.65 and an eight ounce rump with mushrooms, tomatoes and onion rings for £7.65. There is a non-smoking restaurant.

The White Hart has ten rooms for bed and breakfast, prices from £20 to £50 for a family room. There is a patio, background music and winter quiz nights. The pub is open from 10.00 to 23.00. Normal Sunday opening.

THE PLOUGH INN 87

Sway Road, Tiptoe, near Lymington. Tel (01425) 610185

The Plough is a traditional old English inn, built originally as a farm in 1660. The single large through-bar has been decorated in keeping with the Solent Inn image, featuring beams, open gas fire and copper pan lids. The restaurant area is secluded and the huge garden has a good play area for children. Although primarily a local's pub, the Plough attracts a number of tourists from the nearby caravan site. Resident at the pub is a ghost called Jack, but he generally only appears when there are changes at the inn.

This is a Whitbread pub run by Keith and Jacky Spalding and with a reputation for its range of real ales for example Flowers Original, Wadworth 6X, Brakspear Bitter, Boddingtons Bitter and Wethered Winter Royal. Also on draught are Murphys stout, Boddingtons Mild, Guinness, Whitbread Best Bitter, Heineken, Stella Artois and Strongbow cider.

The menu is posted on the blackboard and prices are very reasonable. Choices include ham and mushroom or tuna and mayonnaise garlic melts £2.75, steakwich with fried onion £2.65, cottage pie £3.95, trout with asparagus, croquette potatoes and salad £4.45, seafood pasta and salad £4.45, rump steak £7.95, gammon steak with egg or pineapple £5.25 and seafood platter £5.25. Children's meals £2.15.

There are plenty of organised activities including an air rifle club. Children are welcome in the restaurant area and dogs on leads are allowed in the bar. Credit cards accepted. The Plough is open daily from 11.00 - 23.00 with normal Sunday opening hours.

Hythe Road, Marchwood. Tel (01703) 867752

Amiable proprietor, Ron Longman, converted these 200 hundred-year-old cottages into the delightful, 'olde worlde' Pilgrim Inn, and as you drive into the car park you will be struck by the well maintained, award winning garden (Benson and Hedges UK Pub Garden), neat thatch and healthy hanging baskets. This is a typical, well kept country pub with a real fire, solid oak beams, copper pots, mugs, shields and old photographs of the area. The bar is L-shaped with comfortable velvet seating around the walls providing cosy corners for quiet conversation. You will not find intrusive fruit machines, pool, darts or juke box.

The Pilgrim is a free house offering Worthington Best Bitter, John Smiths Bitter, Guinness, Mild, Tennent's Extra, Tennent's Pilsner, Carling Black Label, Dry Blackthorn and Autumn Gold cider on draught. Real ales are Draught Bass, Courage Best and Directors, Gales Country wines and the inn's own non-alcoholic beer.

The typical pub menu is amongst the cheapest and best value in the area. There is a bar menu, a specials board and a restaurant opposite the pub for evening dining. Choices include sandwiches from £1.40, soup of the day £1.20, ham and mushroom tagliatelle, shepherds pie both £2.25, home-cooked ham £3, prawn open sandwich £3 and desserts, such as syrup sponge and custard, Eves pudding, raspberry russe, toffee and Austrian chocolate gateau £1.75. Three-course table d'hote menu at the Pilgrims Progress restaurant £11.00 but if you prefer á la carte you can choose from starters such as smoked salmon and asparagus mousse £3.50 and king prawns in a white wine, garlic and cream sauce £4.50. Main courses range from grilled halibut steak finished with shelled prawns and garlic butter £9.50 to beef Wellington with red wine and shallot sauce £12.95.

Well behaved dogs are permitted, but children are only allowed inside if eating. The Pilgrim Inn is open 11.00 - 14.30 (15.00 Saturday), 18.00 - 23.00 and normal Sunday hours.

The Cross, Burley. Tel (01425) 403423

Located in the heart of the Forest this small village has become quite a tourist centre, and being the only pub in the village, the Queens Head caters for many of these visitors. The centre part of the pub has been a public house since 1630, and as such is steeped with history, much of it linked with smuggling activities. A smuggler's horse is reputed to be buried near the bar and in recent years pistols, coins and guns have been found buried at the site. It is supposedly haunted by a ghost of a smuggler and one can also see the beginning of a tunnel built between the pub and the manor. A lot of this history is traced in letters and photographs on the walls, along with guns, axes and a large collection of horsebrasses and bits. The bar is warmed by two open log fires. The pub at one time also housed the village forge and some stables.

The Queens Head is a Whitbread Wayside Inn run by Tony and Jane Walton. Whitbread Best Bitter, Flowers Original, Wadworth 6X, Boddingtons Bitter, Murphys stout, Heineken, Stella Artois and Strongbow cider served on draught.

There are several quiet corners throughout the spacious open-plan bar but probably the main feature is the food counter, typical of the Wayside design. A blackboard menu lists a number of wholesome, homemade country dishes and diners take a tray and order dishes from the servery. Typical choices are beef and venison casserole £3.95, braised steak £4.80, layer pie with minced beef, mushrooms, potatoes and cheese layers £3.50 and steak and kidney pudding £3.50 and Burley bake with macaroni, leeks and celery toppped with cheese £3.50.

The Queens Head is open from 11.00 - 23.00 Monday to Saturday and from 12.00 - 22.30 on Sundays. Children, but not dogs are allowed inside. There is live entertainment in winter, otherwise background music fills the bar, which also houses a bar billiards table. There is patio seating and a large car park.

Hightown Road, Ringwood. Tel (01425) 473701

Originally a coach house the Railway is known only to locals and is a friendly, informal, drinker's pub. There is a cosy lounge bar and large, noisier public bar with traditional pub games - darts, dominoes and crib. And in keeping with public house tradition, you will not be confronted with the smell of fried food, in fact no food at all is served.

This is an Eldrige Pope property hosted by Adrian Langdown and Kate Phipps, EP Best Bitter, Hardy Country and 3D Bitter are served on handpump. Tetley Bitter, Guinness, Carlsberg, Carlsberg Export and Dry Blackthorn cider are also on draught.

The Railway is open all day 11.00 - 23.00 six days a week with normal Sunday hours. There is a pretty garden almost obscured by a weeping willow and petanque is played. Bed and breakfast £14.50 per person.

113 High Street, Lymington. Tel (01590) 672276

The decor of this cosy pub has to be described as basic, even scruffy, but I suspect this may be largely the fault of the previous brewery. To me this pub is a delightful, untouched pub probably best visited on Saturday morning as the busy Lymington market bustles right on the doorstep. The locals are almost itching to enter into conversation with you and owners John and Carol Baddock, are very hospitable. We couldn't find very much history to the pub except that the building is Grade II listed and one of the oldest hosteleries in town, and stories of a local bus that ploughed into the front - luckily it was after hours! There is however, a well meaning parrot called Bruno who is known for dive bombing the clientele.

A free house, the Red Lion is renowned for its well kept ales - Fullers London Pride, Marstons Pedigree, Ringwood Best Bitter and Arthur Pendragon - and is featured in the CAMRA Good Beer Guide. Whitbread Best Bitter, Guinness, Heineken, Stella Artois and Stonehouse cider are also on draught. Good selection of rums.

The basic but good value, home-cooked menu features, "basket cases" - which they claim has no reference to the regulars - and includes spiced chicken wings, salad and chips £2.50 and jumbo sausage, chips and salad £1.95. Also featured are spiced pork belly ribs with salad £2.95. cod, chips and peas £3.00, plaice, chips and peas £3.50 - the most expensive item on the menu - and giant Yorkshire pud with various fillings £2.50, and various soups, sandwiches and filled jacket potatoes. Sunday lunches and evening meals are only served in the summer season.

There is an enclosed rear garden area for children and well behaved dogs are welcome inside. B&B at £15 per person. The pub is open all day - 11.00 - 23.00 - six days a week and the normal Sunday hours.

Boldre, near Lymington. Tel (01590) 673177

The Red Lion is a traditional country pub dating back to the 17th century and is a real picture during the summer months with its facade adorned with colourful flower displays. It is close to St. John's Church, famous for the H.M.S. Hood memorial, and Spinners Gardens, which is known for its many rare shrubs. The comfortably furnished interior is festooned with an array of artefacts, including numerous antiques, farm tools, tasteful prints, tapestries, cups, mugs, jugs, plates, warming pans and a collection of man and animal traps!

The pub is owned by Eldridge Pope and dispenses their Royal Oak Bitter, Hardy Country Ale and Dorchester Bitter on handpump, plus EP Best Bitter, Carlsberg, Kronenbourg and Dry Blackthorn cider on draught. Good selection of up to 20 wines by the glass. The Bicknell family, currently John and Penny, have been in charge here for over 22 years.

The weekly changing menu may feature half duckling £6.50, gammon, eggs and chipped potatoes £6.50, vegetable casserole and jacket potato £4.50 and spicy chicken with rice £4.50. Most of the main dishes are reasonably priced at less than £7 except for a few game specials in season. The starters are around £3.50 so a full meal could be more expensive than the average property listed in this guide. Having said that, the smoked fish dish of salmon, mackerel and trout £3.50 was excellent value but the tiny plate of crudities accompanied by brown and tired guacamole £2.00, was not. The service was very willing, friendly, scatty and vague. Desserts are homemade and include fruit pies, gâteaux and cheesecake, priced around £2.50.

The pub is open all day, 11.00 - 23.00 in the summer and 11.00 - 15.00 and 18.00 - 23.00 winter. Normal Sunday hours. There is a patio area and a sheltered garden with a children's climbing frame for summer imbibing. No children under 14 or dogs allowed in the bars.

Market Place, Ringwood. Tel (01425) 474253

This pub contrasts a lively, noisy public bar with a quieter beamed lounge bar and a comfortable family area with children's toys, highchair and television. The bars are delightfully cluttered and covered with posters of all the local goings on. The building dates back 300-400 years, a time when the lounge bar was a shop, but it is possible it has been a local centre for news and frivolity for many years. You can ask to see extracts from the Salisbury and Winchester Journal, dating back to 1813 when the landlord used to brew the beer on the premises.

This is a Greenall property with Whitbread Best Bitter, Newquay Steam Bitter, Guinness, Heineken, Stella Artois and Strongbow cider available on draught. Real ales include Ringwood Fortyniner.

The food is excellent value, typical pub fayre and the portions are generous. Dishes include whitebait £2.25, crispy coated baby mushrooms with garlic dip £2.35, pâté £2.95, sandwiches from 90p, two jumbo sausages £2.90, homemade quiche £2.95, jacket potato with prawns £2.60, ham salad £3.25, Stilton ploughman's £2.95, gammon steak £4.25, fried scampi £3.50 and half roast chicken £4.15. There is a specials board and vegetarian board but top value is a cheap and cheerful selection, including a 5-inch burger with onions and relish 95p and jumbo hotdog and onions £1.50. Sweets include, blackberry and apple pancakes, treacle sponge and custard and homemade fruit pies, all £1.50. Kiddies meals £1.75.

The Red Lion is open from 11.00 - 23.00 every day (Wednesday and Saturday from 10.00) and Sunday normal hours. Families and dogs are welcome and there is a patio and garden with play area. Overnight accommodation £15 per person.

RED ROVER 94

West Wellow, near Romsey. Tel (01794) 322266 ⚔ * "Top Toilets" award

You cannot miss the Red Rover at Wellow, but watch the deadly traffic from the east as you turn off the A36. This village pub-restaurant is 300 years old and has been a coach house, a commoner's court, the village butchers and the homeguard head quarters during World War II. It takes its name from the old coach that travelled the London to Southampton Road. The bar area which still has some of the original stone floor, has historic photographs of Wellow and some of the local characters, as well as generous bar stools shaped like tractor seats.

A Whitbread inn run by Val and Paul Brooker, it dispenses Whitbread Best Bitter, Guinness, Mild, Heineken, Stella Artois and Dry Blackthorn cider on draught, whilst real ale choices include Flowers IPA, Ringwood Best Bitter, Boddingtons Bitter and Wadworth 6X.

There is both a lunchtime and evening menu plus a daily specials board, and one can call in for morning coffee from 10.30am. Reasonably priced standard favourites are offered at lunchtime, while the evening menu specialises in traditional grills such as breaded spicy chicken breast £5.25 and 16oz 'T' bone steak £9.00. Starters include mushroom stroganoff with garlic bread £3.25, butterfly prawns and spicy dip £3.75 and chicken tikka and yoghurt dip £3.25.

The Red Rover opens from 10.30 - 15.00 and 18.30 - 23.00 Monday to Saturday and the normal Sunday hours. Facilities include a pin ball machine, a skittles alley, a garden and the Coach House function room that can be hired for parties and business meetings. Of particular note at the Red Rover are the exceptional loos; exceptional for their high standard of decor and cleanliness. Check them out yourself. Disabled facilities. Children welcome in the dining area. Credit cards accepted.

Toms Lane, Linwood, near Ringwood. Tel (01425) 475792

The Red Shoot dates from 1940 and is a spacious open-plan pub tastefully extended and redecorated in Regency pink with wooden floors, tailored curtains and stuffed animals. Antique furniture, period prints and paintings contribute to the "cared for" look of the pub. It was once the village post office. Situated in a particularly attractive part of the Forest adjacent to a campsite, the pub attracts customers on all forms of transport. There is a hitching rail for riders on horseback.

A managed Wadworth property with Wadworth IPA and 6X, Farmer's Glory, Marston's Merrie Monk, Adnams Southwold Bitter, Hall and Woodhouse Tanglefoot and Bass Draught on handpump. Also served on draught are Toby Bitter, John Smiths Bitter, Beamish stout, Castlemaine XXXX, Heineken, Stella Artois, Dry Blackthorn and Red Rock cider. There is also a good selection of reasonably priced country fruit wines including parsnip, dandelion and damson.

Food is served every session and includes a popular roast on Sunday lunchtimes. The menu includes sandwiches from £1.50, prawns on a bed of lettuce £2.75, chicken wings Cajun style £2.75, double jumbo sausage, egg and fries £2.95, homemade chilli £3.95, deep-fried breaded scampi £4.95, sizzling steaks from £7.95 and the popular foresters lunch £2.95 which includes a bowl of homemade soup served with a chunk of crusty bread, salad, sweet pickle and pickled onions and either cheddar cheese, Stilton or pâté. There is also a daily specials board and food is served up to 22.00 at weekends.

The Red Shoot is open all day 11.00 - 23.00 in the summer, normal Sunday hours and, 11.00 - 15.00 and 18.00 - 23.00 in the winter. Children are welcome in the comfortable family room. Easy access and toilet for the disabled. There is live entertainment on Sunday nights.

RISING SUN INN 96

Bashley Common Road, Wootton, near New Milton. Tel (01425) 610360

Situated on the edge of a wide expanse of New Forest, the original inn is listed in the Domesday Book and is therefore marked in Ordnance Survey maps. The current building dates around 1900 and has just undergone major refurbishment. The carpeted family dining area is decorated neatly in a Victorian style and the less formal bar area has been designed to reflect the rural position of the pub with old photographs from the New Forest museum, saddles and bric-a-brac.

The pub is owned by Whitbread and tenanted by Steve Croll. Five traditional real ales are served and will include a selection of Flowers Original, Boddingtons Bitter, Wadworth 6X, Brakspear, Strong Country Bitter and Castle Eden Ale. Guinness, Heineken, Stella and Strongbow cider are also available on draught.

The Rising Sun offers typical pub fayre at reasonable prices. Dishes include chef's soup of the day £1.45, hot mushrooms served with a choice of dips £2.25, vegetable parcels £2.75, chicken satay £2.95, steak n' kidney pudding £4.75, braised venison £4.95, lamb and apricot casserole £5.25, half a roast chicken £4.50, beef and Guinness pie £5.50, 8oz sirloin steak £8.25, gammon steak £4.95, lasagne verdi £4.75, fillet of plaice £3.95, fish pie £5.25, freshly made ham salad £4.75 and a light platter of salmon mousse and bread £3.50. Sweets are priced around £2.00 and include gâteaux, cheesecakes and fruit pies. There is a large garden with potbellied pigs, a pony, donkeys and goats, and ample car parking. Traditional pub games such as crib and dominoes. Dogs, horses and children are welcome. Disabled toilets, nappy changing facilities and high chairs.

Opening hours are from 11.00 - 23.00 Monday to Saturday. A full menu is offered all day, every day. Normal Sunday licensing hours. Major credit cards accepted. Two double en-suite rooms with lovely Forest views available from £39.50.

ROCKINGHAM ARMS 97

Canada Road, West Wellow, near Romsey. Tel (01794) 322473

Ideally situated for walks into the Forest, The Rock, as it is affectionately known, is a family run, traditional country pub with two bars, a 50-seater restaurant and a children's play area. It was built in the late 19th century as a chapel but was never used for worship and is now named after the local brickworks. The beams, fireplaces and stone floor in the Forest bar all help to make this a very popular pub with the locals and anyone else lucky enough to discover it.

The Rock is a free house run by Paul and Wendy Broomfield. Regular ales on handpump include, Courage Best Bitter, Rock Special Brew and Best Bitter, plus Websters Yorkshire Bitter, Worthington Best Bitter, Guinness, Fosters, Kronenbourg, Budweiser, Labatt's, Hofmeister and Dry Blackthorn cider on draught. There is always a good selection of guest real ales posted on a blackboard along with their strengths. They may include Draught Bass, Charles Wells Bombardier, Wadworth 6X, Ringwood Fortyniner and Hook Norton Best Bitter.

There is a full time chef and we found the food to be faultless. The reliable bar menu includes sandwiches or rolls from £1.50, button mushrooms served in a cream, garlic, herb and wine sauce £1.95, cottage pie topped with grated cheese £3.75, beef, ale and mushroom pie £4.75, beef curry with rice, pappadoms and mango chutney £3.75, and rump steak with mushrooms, grilled tomato, vegetables and French fries £7.75. Children's menu £1.95.

The Rock is open from 11.45 - 14.30 Monday to Wednesday, 11.30 Thursday and Friday, 11.15 - 15.00 Saturday, and 18.00 - 23.00, (from 17.30 Fridays).

Rockbourne, near Fordingbridge. Tel (017235) 236

The Rose and Thistle is a very pretty, 17th century, thatched pub in the idyllic Hampshire village of Rockbourne. The civilised lounge bar acts as the restaurant and the public bar is a beamed room with inglenook fireplace, flag stone floors and prints of gentleman's sports. The pub is charming with country-style fabrics, oak tables, carved settles, benches and dried flowers. It appears well run and the bar person, Jacky, was extremely helpful.

The pub is a free house owned by a conglomerate of fifteen people. Courage Best, Directors, John Smiths Bitter, Wadworth 6X, Kronenbourg, Fosters, Guinness and Dry Blackthorn cider are served on draught.

The food is a little expensive but justified by its quality, the polite service and ambience. The menu certainly leaves your mouth watering. Some choice selections included mushroom pot - button mushrooms sautéed with smoked bacon, cream and brandy, topped with gruyere cheese and browned £3.25, scrambled eggs, smoked salmon and prawns £4.50, sautéed soft herring roes on toast £2.65, baked seafood pancake £4.95, Barnsley chop - a double lamb chop grilled to order with potatoes and vegetables £7.25, and for sweet, petit pot a la creme - a rich creamy baked custard flavoured with caramel, coffee, vanilla and dark chocolate at £2.95.

Despite the upmarket look of the pub they do offer occasional live entertainment. There is a well kept garden at the front of the pub and a car park at the rear. The Rose and Thistle is open 11.00 - 15.00 and 18.00 - 23.00 and normal Sunday hours. Credit cards accepted.

Lyndhurst Road, Brockenhurst. Tel (01590) 22225

Situated in the rural village of Brockenhurst, this hotel has lost much of its original charm by trying to cater to a mass market. The bar is however lively, especially at New Forest Show time (last week in July), and spacious. A large well kept beer garden is open in the summer.

The Rose and Crown is serviced by Eldridge Pope, and Hardy Country, Dorchester Bitter and Royal Oak are on handpump. Tetley Bitter, Castlemaine 4X, Kronenbourg, Guinness and Dry Blackthorn cider are also on draught.

There is a large servery and food is in the medium to upper pub price bracket with starters from £2.65 and Mexican specialities from £6.25.

The Rose and Crown is open all day 11.00 - 23.00 with normal Sunday hours. Accommodation is reasonably priced from £19.50 single and £44 double.

Downton, near Lymington. Tel (01590) 642297

This is a clean, crisp, neat, predictably traditional pub with three real fires and a non-smoking bar. Freshly polished accoutrements decorate the fireplaces and horse brasses, pots, tools, guns and harness hang on the walls. The pub seems oblivious to modern Whitbread trends and is recommended by Egon Ronay. The pub was established in 1695 and run by the same family for the past 135 years. There is a family portrait in the bar. The oak tree at the front, which appears to grow out of the walls and forecourt, was used to secure horses in the days when this was an important staging post from Bournemouth.

Real ales are Ringwood Best Bitter, Wadworth 6X and Flowers Original. Whitbread Best Bitter, Guinness, Heineken, Stella Artois and Stonehouse cider are on draught.

Lighter bites start at £1.80 and include garlic bread with cheese, and a Bosun's plate of smoked mackerel with granary bread and horseradish. More substantial dishes are all priced at £4.70 and include cottage pie, beef lasagne, chicken curry, fisherman's hot pot and a good choice of vegetarian dishes. Excellent sweets priced from £2.50. Blackboard specials.

Landlady, Audrey Everleigh pointed out the well maintained garden with children's entertainment and view over the distant cliff tops. There is a family room but children under 14 are not allowed in the bars. Dogs also not permitted. Car park at rear. No juke boxes or fruit machines. Disabled access.

The Royal Oak is open 11.30 - 14.30ish and 18.30 - 23.00 in the winter and 23.00 - 15.00 and 18.00 - 23.00 in the summer. Normal Sunday hours.

Fritham. Tel (01703) 812606

The partly thatched Royal Oak is rustic in every sense of the word and has an earthy time-warp quality all of its own, being as it is one of the few remaining unspoilt, rural gems. Set in a delightfully location in the heart of the Forest it is close to Eyeworth Pond and is an ideal spot to begin a walk. There is no food - except the occasional barbecue - and no frills. The decor being primitive with wood panelled walls, plastic chairs and benches. There is a tiny snug bar with a wide-arched open fireplace, pews, pots, wooden beams, kettles and wellington boots dumped as the landlord's children walk through from the stables. The only concession to the 20th century is the fruit machine.

Andrew and Eileen Taylor who now own the pub are the third generation and would like the pub to stay as close as it can to when it was a popular smugglers pub in the 18th century. Situated on the "Smugglers Way", those moving goods from the water for auction under cover of the forest, stopped at the pub for refreshments. Forest workers gave the smugglers a hand in return for cheap liquor and tea.

The real ales - Marston's Pedigree, Strong Country Bitter and Ringwood Best Bitter - are drawn straight from the barrels behind the bar, and also available on draught are Whitbread Best Bitter, Mild, Guinness, Heineken and Dry Blackthorn cider.

The Royal Oak is open from 11.00 - 15.00 and 18.00 - 23.00 and the normal Sunday hours. There is a garden with caged birds and the pub is also a working smallholding so be prepared to push pigs or chickens out of the way as you cross the yard to the toilets.

Ringwood Road, North Gorley, Fordingbridge. Tel (01425) 652244

* "Don't Miss" award

The Royal Oak is a pretty, 17th century thatched New Forest pub. Picturesquely set opposite a splendid oak, and a duck pond, the Royal Oak is a "real pub serving food" and ably run by Ron and Vee Newsham who aim to cater for all tastes. Two traditionally furnished bars - Acorn and Oakleaf - boast oak beams, panels, warming open fires, low ceilings and are simply furnished and decorated. Here we found the most convincing evidence concerning the presence of an active ghost. Hannah has been there since the 1700's and she is a friendly but very mischievous ghost who likes drawing attention to herself.

A Whitbread pub dispensing Flowers Original, Ringwood Best Bitter and a guest ale such as Brakspear Bitter on handpump. Whitbread Best Bitter, Trophy, Murphys stout, Guinness, Stella Artois, Heineken and Stonehouse cider are also on draught.

There is a happy kitchen serving typical pub fayre at medium prices. The menu board changes daily but includes starters like garlic mushrooms £2.95 and game soup £1.95 and vegetarian dishes such as leek and potato mornay and spinach, mushroom and tomato bake both £4.50 Also available are ploughman's £3.50, steak and ale pie with kidney, steak and Stilton pie £5.25, seafood gratin £5.25, lamb curry £4.95, cottage pie £4.50, local ham, egg and fries £4.25, beef lasagne £4.95, barbecue ribs £5.50 and ribeye steak with all the trimmings £7.50. Sweets include homemade specials such as spotted dick, sherry, apple trifle, apple crumble, treacle tart, all £1.75, and pecan and toffee cheesecake £2.50.

The Royal Oak is open 11.00 - 14.30 (15.00 Saturdays) and 18.00 - 23.00 weekdays and normal Sunday hours. Children are not allowed in the bars but there is a family room with pool table, darts, dominoes and crib, and a beer garden with swings and climbing apparatus. There is a juke box in the Oakleaf bar. Dogs are allowed inside on a lead. Coaches welcome.

Hill Top, Beaulieu. Tel (01590) 612228

Built in the early 1800's, the Royal Oak was originally two smallholdings and enjoys a splendid position with views across the heathland with Fawley refinery in the distance. There is one long, semi-circular bar with plastered walls, pot plants and tidy, neatly laid tables and pictures of Forest scenes. Well run by Pam and Paul Roberts, it is a friendly establishment, and popular with both tourists and local Esso staff. It is handy for visitors to the 200-acre Exbury Gardens on the east bank of Beaulieu River, which apart form the world-famous Rothschild collection, has woodland walks, heather gardens, ponds and a daffodil meadow.

Owned by Whitbread one will find Morland Old Speckled Hen, Strong Country Bitter, Flowers Original and Boddingtons Bitter on handpump plus Whitbread Best Bitter, Guinness, Heineken, Stella Artois and Strongbow cider on draught.

The medium priced lunchtime bar menu emphasises healthy eating and includes filled baps from £2.95, filled jacket potatoes with salad from £4.75, cod, prawn and broccoli pie £4.95, chicken in yoghurt, and orange sauce £4.95, chilli con carne £4.75 and ploughman's £3.95. The evening meal features prawn and pineapple cocktail £3.25, chicken breast salad £5.75, sizzling platter of teriyaki beef £5.25 and speciality grilled sirloin steak £9.95. Children's dishes are also more healthy than the normal pub favourites but also a little more pricey. There is a no smoking area.

The Royal Oak is open 11.00 - 15.00 and 18.00 - 23.00 and normal Sunday hours. Children are not allowed in the bar unless they are dining but are well catered for outside with a large garden with a chalet, playground, telephone box and pot-bellied pigs. There is ample space in the memorably treacherous car park.

THE RYDAL 104

93 Station Road, New Milton. Tel (01425) 610619

You can always spot a real "locals" pub, you almost get trampled in the eleven o'clock rush. At the time when most of us would be sitting down to morning coffee the friendly barmaid of this two-bar pub is pulling high-speed pints. Built as a private house in 1886, the Rydal came to life in 1941 and is located one mile from the Forest, one mile from the sea and close to the High Street shops. Cheerful landlady Gladys Walker has been here 44 years, experiencing three different brewery owners and will definitely give you a warm welcome. There is a huge lively public bar and a warmer lounge with unobtrusive piped music and an adjacent velvet snug room. Decor is red with striped wallpaper and fairy lights.

The Rydal is a Whitbread pub serving two real ales namely Flowers Original, and a guest beer, usually Ringwood Best Bitter or Brakspear Bitter. Whitbread Best and Poacher, Murphys stout, Guinness, Heineken, Stella Artois and Strongbow cider are also on draught.

The menu offers typical pub grub at unbeatable prices. Items include cottage pie £2.95, scampi £3.95, cod fillet in batter £3.95, chicken curry £3.50, fisherman's pie £2.95, pot roast £2.95, lasagne £3.25, ham and egg £2.50, smuggler's pie £2.95 and steak and kidney pie £3.95, all of which are served with chips or jacket potato, peas and carrots. Other favourites range from spaghetti bolognaise £2.50 and sausage and mash £2.50, to ham and mushroom tagliatelle £2.50 and a choice of ploughman's, jacket potatoes and sandwiches from £1.40. Sweets from £1.50.

The Rydal is open from 11.00 - 15.00 and 18.00 - 23.00 and normal Sunday hours. Children are not allowed in the main bar area but there is an attractive garden.

High Street, Fordingbridge. Tel (01425) 652776

The Ship, located in the High Street opposite the Damerham turning, is a real local's pub with both a lounge and spacious public bar. Previously the New Inn, it boasts a very friendly, informal atmosphere. The landlady, Anne Smith, is charming and you will find the locals willing to recount many a story of the area.

This is a Courage pub serving Courage Best Bitter and guest ale, Newport Best Bitter - £1.30 pint - or Cooks New Forest Gold - £1.25 - on handpump. Webster's Green Label Bitter, Guinness, Fosters, Kronenbourg and Carlsberg Export are also on draught.

There is a bar menu and some very cheap pub grub, all of good quality, and carefully prepared. Sandwiches from £1.10, filled jacket potatoes from £1.95, steak sandwich £1.95, ham or cheese ploughman's £2.50, sausage, egg and chips £2.75, steak and kidney pie £3.95, breaded cod, chips and peas £3.50, homemade quiche £3.50, grilled local trout £4.50, homemade lasagne £3.95, mixed grill £5.95 and 8oz rump steak £5.95. The specials board offers homemade dishes such as cheese, leek and ham pie £3.75. Puddings £1.50 range from homemade apple pie and rhubarb crumble to treacle tart and passion cake, all served with custard, cream or icecream. Popular two-course Sunday roast £4.50.

The Ship Inn is open 11.00 - 23.00 weekdays and normal Sunday hours. There is a small garden and free public car park to the rear. Bed and breakfast £15 per person.

Salisbury Road, Plaitford, near Romsey. Tel (01794) 322397

If you manage to negotiate the busy main road between the car park and the front door, your bravery will be well rewarded. The Shoe is a very friendly pub, steeped with history and should not be missed on a visit to the Forest. Built in 1520, the Shoe Inn took its name from the cavalry troops who frequented it when travelling from the garrison in Salisbury to the port of Marchwood. The timber framed front was added in 1711 when the inn became a posting station for mail coaches. A toll-gate was constructed across the road and the landlord made responsible for collecting the King's tolls.

The last New Forest highwayman, John Taylor, was caught while drinking at the pub and publicly hanged on the nearby Plaitford Common. Queen Victoria who stopped here on route to the Isle of Wight.

Landlord Robin Huntley alias "Smiler" used to work with the comedian-magician, Tommy Cooper, and can be persuaded, probably for not much more than a gin and tonic, to perform some of his tricks, some of them using the star's original props.

The Shoe is a free house and has a good selection of draught beers and lagers, which may include John Smiths Bitter, Courage Best Bitter, Guinness, Beamish, Mild, Fosters and Kronenbourg. Real ales change regularly, but usually include Fullers London Pride, Wadworth 6X, and a Ringwood brew.

Cheap pub grub is served at lunchtime only, the menu featuring toasted sandwiches from £1.45, homemade thick vegetable soup £1.95, large jacket potato with cheese or beans £1.95, super ploughman's £2.50, deep fried garlic mushrooms with salad £3.50 and beef or chicken curry £3.50.

Dogs are not welcome in the bar, well behaved children are away from the bars and there is a small garden for summer days. Pool, darts and dominoes. The Shoe opens from 11.00 - 15.00ish, 19.00 - 23.00 and all day Saturday.

The Quay, Lymington. Tel (01590) 676903

   The Ship Inn has clearly the best location in Lymington, right on the quay at the bottom of the picturesque cobbled lane from the High Street (there is a pay and display car park opposite), and overlooking Lymington River and its marinas. Also in its favour are the stone floors, its cave like bars and the decidedly yachty clientele, all of which are not typical of a Brewers Fayre property. The blue sweaters, sailing trousers, designer footwear and the presence of shower facilities, are more indicative of some exclusive sailing club. The pub's identity is probably only given away by the corporate menus. As one would expect for its location, the Ship is a popular destination at all times and you will find the very active and energetic manager, Paul Congdon, very helpful.
   Real ales on offer are Wadworth 6X, Flowers Original and Boddingtons Bitter. Also on draught are Whitbread Best, Heineken, Heineken Export, Stella Artois and Strongbow cider.
   With a Brewers Fayre facility you can be confident of reasonably priced food all day. Orders are taken at the counter once you have a table number. Starters are priced from £1.15 and include the inevitable soup, pâté and prawn cocktail. Light bites include an excellent value steak Hoagie, a grilled slice of sirloin steak served with onions in a wholemeal roll £2.95. "Hot platters" range from steak and kidney pie £3.95, half a roast chicken £4.70 and fish pie £4.75 to fillet of salmon £5.95 and sole Bearnaise £5.25. Vegetable dishes, savoury dishes, salad platters and sandwiches are also available. Sunday roasts £4.95. Good value Vin de Pays at £4.95.
   There is a patio area with a memorable view over the river. Children welcome, but no dogs. Access and Visa cards. Open all day from 11.00 - 23.00 except Sunday when normal licensing hours apply, but food can be ordered from 12 noon to 22.00.

Old Romsey Road, Cadnam. Tel (01703) 812236

The Sir John Barleycorn is a long and low, thatched, inn dating back to the 12th century and, according to licensees Trevor and Delores Lamb is reputed to be one of the oldest in Hampshire. The building was originally two cottages, one of them belonging to Punkiss the woodcutter who found the body of King Rufus. It is no longer on the main road but you can see a sign at exit 1 off the M27 at the entrance to the New Forest. There are three, attractive and comfortable, music and game-free bars, the top one laid for diners and controlled children. There is an open fire, original beams and low ceilings and various pictures adorn the walls including viws of the pub in different seasons. The pub is popular with a generally upmarket clientele and the new breed of lunchtime diners.

It is a Whitbread pub offering Whitbread Best, Guinness, Heineken, Stella Artois and Strongbow cider on draught, plus three real ales namely Flowers Original, Strong Country Bitter and a guest brew.

The inn has always had a reputation for quality food but a new improved menu is being published and blackboard specials posted following the arrival of the new licensees. "Tempters" include soup of the day £1.60, prawns served hot in blue cheese sauce £3.60, farmhouse pâté £2.95 and smoked peppered mackerel £2.50. Main courses range from beefsteak pie £4.95, chicken and mushroom pie £4.95, homemade ham and mushroom quiche £4.55 and fried scampi with tartare sauce £5.75, to prawn salad platter £5.75, two cheese ploughman's £3.30, trout £3.95 and an 8oz sirloin steak at £9.95. Homemade asparagus and Stilton quiche £4.55 may feature on the vegetarian list and fresh lobster and crab are advertised on the blackboard outside in season. Desserts £2.25 include passion cake, chocolate fudge cake and apple pie. The wine list starts at Bordeaux Blanc £9 and includes Sancerre for the connoisseur £16.00.

The Barleycorn is open 11.00 - 15.00 and 18.00 - 23.00 Monday to Saturday and normal Sunday hours. After Easter the pub will be open all day. Dogs are not allowed but there is some bench seating outside between the cars and the pub.

Canterton, near Cadnam. Tel (01703) 813170

This is a traditional country pub to be found off the A31 at the Rufus Stone turning. Although very close to the famous stone marking the spot where King Rufus was shot, the pub only dates back to the early 1900's and is named after his alleged assassin. There is however, a wonderful Forest view and a supervised garden with organised children's games. Inside, you will find a long, thatched bar with several beamed eating areas that are decorated with dried flowers, numerous books and tack, and furnished with pretty curtains and velvet seats.

This is a Courage house run by Surrey Free Inns and managed by Gary and Kareen Ford. Real ales include Courage Directors, Ruddles County, No Name Best Bitter and John Smiths Bitter. Courage Best Bitter, Holsten Export, Kronenbourg, Fosters and Scrumpy Jack cider are also served on draught. Well priced wines.

If you wish to eat it is necessary to find a table and note its number before choosing from five different blackboard menus and from the printed menu and ordering your food from the servery. Starters include a large mushroom filled with tuna and pimento wrapped in filo pastry £2.20 and gazpacho £1.50. The fish menu features grilled trout with prawn and beetroot sauce £5.25 and poached salmon with dill butter £5.50. Other choices include deep fried scampi £4.50, jumbo sausage, fries and beans £2.95 and spicey traders curry £4.50 with half portions for children under ten charged accordingly. Special offers include steak with soup of the day or sweet from £4.99 to £6.99 and a further board advertises the chef's star buys, for example bangers and mash £2.50.

The Sir Walter Tyrrell is open all day from Easter to August, otherwise it closes winter afternoons and opens the normal Sunday hours. There is live entertainment at least once a month, a pianist every Saturday evening and plenty of special events. Children are welcomed away from the bar and dogs, under control. Coaches welcome. Access and Visa accepted.

THE SNAKECATCHER

Lyndhurst Road, Brockenhurst. Tel (01590) 22348

The Snakecatcher is one of the oldest buildings in Brockenhurst, originally being the stables for the horse-drawn coaches that travelled between Lymington and Lyndhurst before the introduction of trains in 1847. The building then became a store before it was converted into an inn, originally named the Railway Inn and designed as a railway carriage.

The pub was renamed in memory of "Brusher" Mills, the snakecatcher who became a famous New Forest character last century. "Brusher" was a "garrulous old hermit" who collected snakes from the Forest and sold many of them to London Zoo. It was not uncommon to see a snake protruding from his pocket and he frequently had one or two in his hands. On one occasion when the pub was crowded with holiday makers and Brusher was having a problem getting attention, he casually threw a couple of snakes on the floor. Everyone scattered, and Brusher was served. In 1905, at the age of 67, Brusher died in the toilet at the pub!

Photographs and news cuttings of "Brusher" adorn the main bar of this friendly, traditional village pub. You will find on handpump, Hardy Country Ale and Royal Oak Strong Ale; with EP Best Bitter, Kronenbourg, Faust, Labatts and Dry Blackthorn cider also available on draught.

Bar snacks include sandwiches £1.20, scampi, seafood platter, plaice, burger, chicken or sausage chips and peas with salad garnish £2.95 to £3.95, ploughman's £2.85, home-cooked specials such as curry and rice or steak and kidney pie £3.50 and sweets such as treacle pudding or chocolate sponge from £1.50. Sunday roasts £3.95 and set 3-course meals £5.95.

The Snakecatcher is open all day during the Summer and on Christmas and New Years Day. Winter hours are 11.00 - 15.00 and 18.00 - 23.00 with the usual Sunday times. There are gardens to side and rear and a popular skittle alley.

THE SPORTSMANS ARMS

South Street, Pennington, near Lymington. Tel (01590) 672585

"Welcome to the Village Pub" is the sign that greets you as you drive from the village square into the spacious car park. And welcome is what landlords Alan and Aileen Pennington would like you to feel. The age of the pub is uncertain but the original walls were mud! The main bar and huge conservatory are decorated in the typical Eldridge Pope style with old tools and glass bottles, there are several booths for private conversation and a convenient ledge below the bar for handbags. There is also a large family room which can be let out for wedding parties and this friendly establishment welcomes disabled people.

The only real ale on hand pump is Royal Oak, otherwise EP Bitter, Carlsberg Pilsner and Export, Labatts and Dry Blackthorn cider are served on draught.

The food is good and reasonably priced. Typical items on the menu are the Sportsman grill with sausage, egg, bacon, mushrooms, beans and hash browns £3.10, beefburger, chips and peas £2.80, quarter chicken £3.25 and mixed grill with a lamb chop, sirloin steak, gammon, sausage, kidney, chips and peas £4.99. Sweets include homemade apple pie and apple crumble, from £1.75. Sunday roast and dessert £4.99. Children's portions from £1.95.

The Sportsmans Arms is open from 11.00 - 14.30 and 18.00 - 23.00, all day Saturday and normal Sunday hours. Children are welcome in the family room inside but no dogs allowed. Bed and Breakfast with TV and tea and coffee making facilities from £13 per person. Coaches are welcome.

THE STAG HOTEL   112

High Street, Lyndhurst. Tel (01703) 283492

Originally built in 1836, the hotel was rebuilt after a fire in 1908. Locals will
delight in recalling the history. Rough plaster, beams and beer mats decorate this
working man's drinking establishment. The locals are friendly and there is
occasional live music.

This is a free house specialising in the locally brewed real ales – Summer
Lightning, Ringwood Best Bitter, Hampshire Lionheart, Hampshire Pendragon
and New Forest Gold.

Basic pub fayre includes venison sausages, jacket potatoes, trout, chips and
peas, burgers and ploughman's from £2.00. Roast of the day £3.75.

The Stag is open 11.00 - 14.30ish and 18.00 - 23.00. Normal Sunday hours. Beer
garden and patio. Bed and breakfast from £17 single and £36 double.

THE STAR INN   113

Market Place, Ringwood. Tel (01425) 473105

There are so many pubs in Ringwood to choose from, but the friendly atmosphere and good food makes the Star popular with the locals in the know. Right in
the centre of town, this pub is packed on market day. There are two cosy bars with
real fires, original beams, local prints, bank notes and mugs in this unspoilt, old
fashioned pub run by a charming landlady, Kate Beeson. The history of the Star is
largely unknown but the lounge bar which is around four hundred years old was
certainly part of a row of houses around the Market Place.

This is a Whitbread property with Best, Guinness, Heineken, Stella Artois and
Strongbow cider on draught. Real ales are Ringwood Best Bitter, Wadworth 6X
and Boddingtons Bitter.

The food is very good but this is a 'real' pub, otherwise known as traditional, so
do not expect evening meals. The menu is carefully thoughout each day, including
a three-course lunch special £5.25. Sandwiches from £1.30, whitebait £3.25,
various filled Yorkshire puddings £2.75, corned beef ploughman's £2.40, cheese,
onion and potato bake £2.50, chilli in potato shells £2.75, chicken, ham and leek
bake £3.25, goujons of plaice £4.25, steak and kidney pudding £4.25 and roast
pork £4.25. Two-course Sunday roast lunch £5.25. Sweets £1.95 include spotted
dick, chocolate sponge, bread and butter pudding, treacle tart and rasberry
pavlova.

The Star is open all day from 10.30 - 23.00 (from 10.00 on Wednesday, market
day) and normal Sunday hours. As this is a comfortable, informal pub, dogs and
children are welcome inside. Games include a skittle alley and darts.

Swan Green, Lyndhurst. Tel (01703) 282203

Situated opposite the picturesque village green, this attractive, 18th century Forest pub has been recently, tastefully refurbished in keeping with local tradition. The dining area has been kept separate from the bar with its wood and stone floors, low beams and cosy armchaired area around real fires. Little history is available but the interior shows a number of old photographs of the area and its people, as well as posters detailing cattle drifts and warning people earlier this century to remove their animals from the roads. The pub, located opposite the local blacksmith, now departed, has its original cob wall front of clay and stones.

The Swan is a Whitbread pub managed by Martin and Clair Burr who serve Whitbread Best Bitter, Murphys stout, Heineken, Stella Artois and Strongbow cider on draught as well as Bulmers Traditional cider from the barrel and the following real ales, Strong Country Bitter, Wadworth 6X and Boddingtons Mild.

This is a Wayside Inn where all the food is home-cooked and pies are a speciality. Dishes include pâté and toast £1.95, deep fried mushrooms with dip £2.25, prawn cocktail £2.95, local sausages £3.95, fried scampi £4.95, fillet of plaice £3.95, fish pie £4.95, 8oz gammon steak £4.95, half roast chicken £4.95, lasagne verdi £4.55, jumbo steak and kidney pudding £4.75, as well as salads, vegetarian dishes - vegetable crumble, mushroom stroganoff, harvesters pie all £4.95 - and light platters from £1.95. The cygnet's menu for children includes soup of the day, crispy vegetable pancake roll, lasagne, fish boat and chicken nuggets; certainly the most innovative and almost verging on healthy.

There is a garden with pigs, goats, ducks and a bouncy castle to keep children amused. Dogs and children are welcomed and the disabled facilities are excellent.

Open from 11.00 - 23.00 every day, including Sunday.

Stuckton, near Fordingbridge. Tel (01425) 652489   * "Good Food" award

The Three Lions is a smart, isolated brick building, now much more a restaurant than a pub and draws discerning clientele from far afield for its cuisine and excellent global wine list. Owners Karl and June Wadsack have spent the last sixteen years developing its reputation resulting in recommendations in many quality guides such as Ackerman and Egon Ronay.

The bar area is small, frequented by locals but is mainly for diners to enjoy a pre-prandial drink. This is a free house offering real ales - Fullers London Pride and Hop Back Summer Lightning on handpump and Guinness, Carlsberg Export and Warsteiner on draught.

The restaurant is divided into discreet dining areas with wine racks, pine tables, copper pots, corn dollies and a relaxed atmosphere. The food is exciting and prepared with care and imagination, but do not expect pub prices. However, compared with top restaurants in the area dishes are still value for money when you have the reassurance that it will be good. The menu is listed on daily changing blackboards and may include New Forest game soup £2.80, carrot, orange and corriander soup £2.80, winter salad with crispy bacon and oak smoked chicken breast £5.30, trio of Swedish herring fillets £4.80, spinach and Gouda strudels £3.90 and warm salad with sauté fresh ducks liver and pine nuts £5.30. Main courses may feature wings of local skate with capers £8.60, roast fillets of Scotch salmon with saffron and lemon sauce £12.20, breast of fresh guinea fowl with sautéed grapes and pine kernels £11.30, fillets of roebuck forestiére with spätzle £12.20 and Scotch fillet steak Café de Paris £14.50. A selection of fresh vegetables or a seasonal salad cost £2.75. Desserts £3.75.

The Three Lions is closed on Sunday, Monday and Bank Holidays, otherwise the bar is open normal pub hours and lunch is served 12.15 - 13.30 and dinner, 19.15 - 21.00 (Saturday till 21.30). Access and Visa accepted. No children under 14 and no dogs.

Ringwood Road, Bransgore. Tel (01425) 72232

The Three Tuns is a picturesque, cosy, thatched pub dating back to the 16th century. There are two low ceilinged, tidy bars featuring exposed beams, panelled walls, two open fires and decorated with gleaming brass ornaments and country bits and pieces. The atmosphere is pleasant and the staff are friendly and helpful.

This is a Whitbread pub with Whitbread Best Bitter, Guinness, Heineken, Stella Artois and Scrumpy Jack cider on draught, and four real ales - Flowers Original, Boddingtons Bitter, Wadworth 6X and Ringwood Best Bitter on hand-pump. There is a good selection of bottled lagers.

The menu is posted on blackboards but the full time chef is very accommodating and will try and pamper to your taste. The dishes change regularly but you will find choices such as oak smoked mackerel £2.50, lambs liver, bacon, onion and mushroom casserole £4.50, homemade steak and kidney pie braised in Guinness £4.75, jumbo sausage, beans and French fries £3.95, tagliatelle in a tomato, garlic and courgette sauce £4.25, scampi with French fries and lemon £4.25 and pan-fried sirloin steak with a black pepper sauce £7.80. Good choice of ploughman's £3.25 and sandwiches from £1.60. Mouthwatering deserts from £2 include spotted dick, banoffee pie, treacle sponge and raspberry ramoss. Special coffee £2.10. The food is almost as spectacular as the hanging baskets that adorn the facade of the pub.

The Three Tuns is set in eleven acres of grounds, has an ample and attractive garden and activities such as barbecues, jazz bands and petanque. Fresh flowers and piped music fills the bars and children and dogs are welcome inside. The pub is open 11.00 - 15.00 and 17.30 - 23.00 Monday to Saturday normal Sunday opening hours. Credit cards accepted.

THE TOLLHOUSE INN   117

167 Southampton Road, Lymington. Tel (01590) 672142

The Tollhouse, "the first pub in Lymington", is possibly the only pub in England with a local heritage museum in the garden. This relates to the nearby ancient settlement of Buckland Rings and is well worth a visit. The pub was the original tollgate into Lymington, but is often referred to as the monkey house, a name which originated in the early 1900's when the landlord kept monkeys at the pub. The interior is mock Tudor in style with plenty of wood-panelling and beams and it is decorated with numerous chamber pots. Your hosts are Geoff and Sueling Emms.

Four real ales may include Ringwood Best Bitter, Tollhouse Special Brew, Boddingtons and Wadworth 6X. Also on draught are Whitbread Best Bitter, Guinness, Murphys stout, Heineken, Heineken Export, Stella Artois and Strongbow cider.

Lunch time bar snacks include ploughman's from £3.60, garlic bread from 95p, open sandwiches from £2.25, filled jacket potatoes from £2.00 and Tollhouse tasties such as bacon and salad baquettes £2.75. The main menu includes an unusual mix of Oriental cuisine and traditional pub food. Try the stir fry and Cantonese starters, chicken cooked with spinach and Amaretta sauce £6.95.

The Tollhouse is open from 11.00 - 15.00 and 18.00 - 23.00 with the usual hours on Sunday. Dogs are not allowed in the lounge bar but children are very welcome in the family room. Winter pub games and live entertainment every Sunday evening from October to April. Garden and museum. Credit cards are accepted.

THE TRAVELLERS REST   118

Hart Hill, Frost Lane, Hythe. Tel (01703) 842356   * "Don't Miss" award

The Traveller's Rest is a truly traditional pub located at the end of a single track road on the edge of Hythe. If you drive out of Hythe along Shore Road into Frost Lane you will see a sign to the pub at the Hart Hill Fork. The pub is at the end of the road at the top of the hill with a wonderful view over the valley below. The Solent Way footpath runs past the front door.

Inside, one steps down into the cosy lounge or the public bar, which landlord Tim Watton and his wife Cheryl, have redecorated in an "old Hythe" theme with photographs of the old town. The trade is mainly local as a result of the discrete location but adventurous visitors are made very welcome. There are splendid views over the valley from the garden, ideal for summer alfresco drinking. Activities at the pub include barbecues, Morris men, October pumpkin competition and summer fun, such as Punch and Judy, for children.

Owned by Whitbread it serves Ringwood Best Bitter, Flowers Original and at least one other real ale on handpump, such as Boddingtons Bitter. Also available on draught are Whitbread Best Bitter, Guinness, Murphys stout, Heineken, Stella Artois, Inches Traditional Scrumpy and Bulmers cider.

Food is served daily except Sunday evening and there is a full range of dishes to choose from. Snacks include filled baguettes £2.25, 4oz burgers with a choice of toppings £1.95 and corn on the cob with garlic butter £1.95. More substantial meals listed are Traveller's pork chop with barbecue sauce £4.95, crispy whitebait with salad £3.50, Italian seafood platter £4.95, homemade specials such as turkey curry £4.75, steak and kidney pie £4.75, courgette and pasta bake £3.95 and beef and Guinness pie £4.75. Sunday roast lunch £4.75. Opening hours are 11.00 - 15.00 and 18.00 - 23.00 (occasionally all day in summer) and normal Sunday hours. Children and dogs are welcome.

Village Green, Minstead, near Cadnam. Tel (01703) 812137

Ye Olde Trusty Servant is a Victorian Inn, tastefully refurbished, and set away from the main roads on one of the most attractive Forest greens. The sign outside the pub depicts "a trusty servant" and a 16th century saying which is believed to originate from Winchester College in the days when the pupils had personal servants, and was possibly the first recorded job description of the staff required. There is a typical Forest bar, sparse with wooden flooring, and two comfortable dining areas for those who appreciate good food and wine in a pleasant ambience.

Owned by Whitbread and run by Gary and Fay Derrick this popular pub dispenses Boddingtons Bitter, Wadworth 6X, and a guest brew such as Hop Back Dry Wheat Ale on handpump. Also on draught are Whitbread Best Bitter, Guinness, Heineken, Stella Artois and Strongbow cider. Well priced house wine.

Chef, "Black Norman", directs the kitchens of the Trusty Servant, contributing to its reputation for a high standard of cuisine. The restaurant is attractive and ideal for a special night out. A printed menu lists pub favourites, including potato skins £3.95, smoked mackerel with horseradish and crusty bread £3.50, local grilled trout £6.95, traditional lasagne £4.95, mushroom omelette £3.95 and Cumberland sausage with chips £3.75. However, there is an extensive and exciting specials board featuring such dishes as monkfish with spinach and cheese £8.95, sea bass in a caper cream sauce £12.95, sizzling rump steak in a hot and spicy sauce £12.45, quails in a blackcurrant and brandy sauce £7.95 and Norman bouillabaisse £10.25.

The inn has six en-suite bedrooms £19.95 single room, a pianist on Saturday evenings and welcomes both children and dogs inside. The bar is open 11.00 - 15.00 and 18.00 - 23.00 and the normal Sunday hours.

Burgate, Fordingbridge. Tel (01425) 652227

The Tudor Rose is a delightful, half-timbered and thatched 14th century free house, located just north of Fordingbridge. This is a well managed, relaxed eating house owned by John and Lyn Butler. Although largely original with flagstones, splendid double-breasted 15th century fireplace and heavy beams, the bar area has been opened up, furnished in red and decorated with many prints and paintings so that very little wall space remains. Most of the doors have been removed due to the ghost, a Cavalier slain by the Roundheads, who is said to knock on doors, only to slam them noisily behind him.

Real ales are well kept and include Ringwood Best Bitter, Wadworth 6X, and a guest ale such as Morland Old Speckled Hen or Brakspear Bitter. Whitbread Best Bitter, Murphys stout, Heineken, Stella Artois and Strongbow cider are also on draught. Gales Country wines.

The blackboard menu is innovative and may include garlic mushrooms £2.50, prawn cocktail £2.95, ploughperson's from £3.25, seafood quiche and salad £3.95, home-made chilli with garlic bread £4.25, chicken Kiev £5.50, 8oz gammon steak with pineapple, peas and salad £5.95, mixed grill £8.95 and chicken breast cooked with a leek and Stilton sauce £5.50. Sunday roasts £4.95. Sweets £2.25 are home-made and include the usual tortes, cheesecakes and a delicious charlotte russe.

There is always plenty going on at the popular Tudor Rose with quiz nights barbecues, darts and promotional nights, and situated as it is on the main Fordingbridge to Salisbury road the pub attracts both passers-by and a good local clientele. Children and dogs are allowed away from the bar area. Attractive beer garden at the front and a larger garden to the rear overlooking fields. Coaches are welcome by appointment. Credit cards accepted. Les Routiers recommended.

Opening hours are from 11.00 - 15.00 and 18.00 - 23.00 and normal Sunday hours.

Main Road, East Boldre, near Beaulieu. Tel (01590) 612331

* Runner-up "Pub of the Year"

Right in the middle of the forest, the Turfcutters succeeds in being not only the village local but a busy and up and coming business pub. It is a picturesque, old fashioned and rustic, forest pub offering excellent service and arguably the best food and bed and breakfast in the New Forest. Pip (from Hobler fame - see entry under Battramsley) has turned the property into a comfortable pub with three cosy, tastefully refurbished rooms, each with a warming open fire. Welcoming touches also include free matches and expected eccentricities such as writing on the wall.

Being a Whitbread pub you will find the normal real ales - Flowers Original, Wadworth 6X and a regularly changing guest ales such as Bunces Old Smokey. Also on draught are Guinness, Mild, Heineken, Stella Artois and Scrumpy Jack cider.

The food is excellent and the menu is similar to that available at the Hobler. Typical main courses include ploughsalad, a choice of Cheddar, Stilton, red Leicester, brie, ham, pâté or mackerel with salad and pickles £3.75, half a shoulder of lamb roasted with rosemary, with minted gravy and fresh vegetables £6.95, chunks of venison marianated in green peppercorn and mushroom sauce £7.95, roast breast of duck served on a sizzling skillet with port and rasberry sauce £10.95 and "sodbashers", Brie and Cambazola wrapped in filo pastry, baked and served with tomato and herb sauce and a mixed salad £4.95. House wine is reasonably priced, as is the popular two pint jug of Cote du Rhone £9.95.

The pub has background music, a large garden, welcomes dogs but not children under 14 in the bar. Most major credit cards are accepted. En-suite overnight accommodation and an enormous breakfast £39 - £45 double. The Turfcutters is open from 11.00 - 14.30 and 18.00 - 23.00 and the normal Sunday hours.

New Forest Heathlands Hotel, Romsey Road, Ower. Tel (01703) 814333

Attached to the Heathlands Hotel the Vine is a 16th century listed building situated just off junction 2 of the M27. It lies on the edge of the New Forest, close to a number of attractions; turn left to Broadlands or right for Paulton's Park.

The Vine, managed by Mike Worley, is frequented both by hotel guests and locals. The bar is snug with original beams, settles, barrel tops, horse brasses and a huge, open fireplace.

As a free house there is a good selection of ales from a diverse range of brewers. At the time of visiting real ales included Ind Coope Burton Ale, Ringwood Best Bitter, Wadworth 6X and Tetley Bitter. Worthington Best Bitter, Guinness, Mild, Lowenbrau, Carlsberg, Carlsberg Export and Gaymers Old English Cyder were on draught. Prices are generally below average.

Food prices are also extremely reasonable and the small but varied menu includes spicy chicken samosas £1.60, homemade soup of the day £1.55 and deep fried broccoli florets £1.55 for starters. Main courses include homemade steak and kidney pie £3.60, deep fried battered cod £3.70, jacket potato longboats £2.45 chinese style BBQ spare ribs £3.35 and vegetable chilli served in taco shells at £2.75. Sandwiches are all £1.45 and a three cheese ploughman's just £2.75. Desserts £1.25.

There is an annexe for children, a juke box and dartboard. Opening hours are 12 noon - 14.30 and 17.00 - 23.00 and normal Sunday hours. En-suite accommodation starts at £40 for a budget room, standard single £63, standard double £77 and residents licence till 01.00. Dogs are not allowed in the bar.

Undershore Road, Lymington. Tel (01590) 672517

The Waggon and Horses is a modernised, country-style pub situated close to the Isle of Wight ferry terminal on Lymington River. Originally called the Waggon Ale House, the deeds of the building date back to 1643. In September 1893 the pub witnessed a shooting tragedy when local gamekeeper, Henry Card proved, unwittingly, that it was possible to shoot oneself in the back. A plaque on the wall records that 'he left a widow and nine orphans'! This is a "grown up's" pub with conservative decor, fish tank and background music.

The Waggon and Horses is owned by Wadworth and run by Mike and Deana Stevens. Real ales on handpump are Bass and Wadworth 6X with John Smiths Bitter, Beamish, Dark Mild, Castlemaine 4X, Kronenbourg, Dry Blackthorn cider and Premium Autumn Gold also on draught.

The menu is a typical pub menu at pub prices and includes a daily specials board. Dishes include egg mayonnaise £2, pâté and toast £2.95, ploughman's from £2.25, sandwiches from £1.50, vegetarian dishes, omelette and salad £4.20, vegetable curry rice £4.95 - chicken Kiev £5.25, beef, prawn and chicken curry £4.95, steak and kidney pie £4.30, filled jacket potatoes from £2.00, lemon sole £5.20 and sirloin steak for £7.75. The specials board may list steak and kidney pudding £3.20, seafood platter £4.95 and half-shoulder of lamb £6.95. Smaller portions for children. Spotted dick and hot crumble fudge cake appear on the pudding list for £2.00.

Open from 11.00 - 14.30 (15.00 Saturdays) and 18.00 - 23.00 weekdays, and normal Sunday hours. There is a pretty patio with bench tables. Children are welcome but dogs are not allowed inside the bar.

THE WATERLOO ARMS   124

Pikes Hill, Lyndhurst. Tel (01703) 282113

Situated behind the Police station just off the main Cadnam to Lyndhurst road, the Waterloo Arms is a three hundred year old, thatched pub that has been in the same family 35 years. In fact the pub has been run by just three families in the last 118 years. The walls are decorated with firearms, spears and a collection of stuffed wildlife, including crocodile, pike and snake. The pub is a typical well run, dark but not gloomy, Forest pub with original beams and an open fireplace.

Despite being a Whitbread tenancy there is an interesting selection of real ales, Boddingtons Bitter, Gales HSB, Flowers Original, Strong Country Bitter and Wadworth 6X. Mild, Guinness, Heineken, Heineken Export and Strongbow cider are also on draught.

The menu is popular with local businessmen; it is imaginative, medium priced and home prepared. The pub still cooks its own ham and the service is good. Typical items listed on the blackboards include fresh mussels cooked in wine, garlic and cream £4.75, toasted sandwiches from £1.60, ploughman's £2.90, sirloin steak sandwich served in fresh bread with salad £4.95, deep fried Camembert with redcurrant and port jelly served with salad and crusty bread £5.25, scampi served with salad and fries £4.95, King prawns with garlic butter and garlic bread £5.45 and tuna fish steak £6.95. Children's menu includes beefburgers, sausages, fish fingers and chicken nuggets served with fries, jacket potato, baked beans or peas, or salad £2.25. The sweet menu boasts toffee and apple pie, cheesecake, profiteroles, all at £2.00 and "Scotch mist", a delicious concoction of meringue, whisky, ice cream and Drambuie.

There is a large, well kept garden and a discretly placed adventure playground. Large car park at the rear. Opening hours are 11.00 - 15.00 and 18.00 - 23.00 weekdays and normal Sunday hours.

THE WHITE BUCK INN   125

Bisterne Close, Burley. Tel (014253) 2264

The White Buck is discretly located to the east of twee and touristy Burley, close to the golf course. Beyond the hotel foyer with its elegant glass doors decorated with "white bucks" lie three plushly decorated rooms with open fires and views across the lawns and gardens set away in the Forest. The pub is equally popular with both locals, walkers and visitors to the hotel.

This is a comfortable free house run by Michael and Brenda Watts. Real ales available are Brakspear Bitter, Ringwood Best Bitter and Wadworth 6X. Worthington Best Bitter, Toby Bitter, Guinness, Murphys stout, Carling Black Label, Heineken, Stella Artois and Dry Blackthorn cider are also served on draught.

The bar menu is posted on a blackboard and changes according to what is in season. A typical selection may include sandwiches from £1.95, pâté and toast £2.50, pint of prawns with brown bread and butter £3.95, hot chilli chicken wings and sour cream dip £3.95, poached fresh salmon, salad and new potatoes £7.25, grilled Avon trout with almonds, peas and new potatoes £6.95, steak, mushroom and Guinness pie £5.25, venison forestiére £6.95, chargrilled steaks from £7.50 and a range of sweets from £2.75. A separate restaurant menu is also available.

There is a family room for children and dogs are welcome. Credit cards except Diners and Amex. The pub is open 11.00 - 14.30 and 18.00 - 23.00 with the normal Sunday hours. En-suite accommodation with Sky TV from £45 single or double.

Romsey Road, Cadnam. Tel (01703) 812277

Built around 1800 this popular local has been recently refurbished to a very high standard, and as with all the properties the Emberley family have been involved with in the Forest, offers a high standard of pub cuisine. Plenty of beams, wooden flooring, brick walls, open fireplace and the inevitable stag heads provide the predictable decor.

Real ales are Flowers Original, Old Speckled Hen, Whitbread Summer Ale and Wadworth 6X. Whitbread Best, Guinness, Murphys stout, Heineken, Stella Artois and Scrumpy Jack are also on draught. Prices are above average.

The only frozen item that is bought by the White Hart is ice cream. All the other ingredients are fresh. The menu includes soup of the day £2.50, chicken liver gâteau with Cognac sauce £4.25, Stilton filled pear with lemon and mint sauce £3.75, chicken and spring onion satay, peanut sauce £3.75, scampi £6.25, vegetarian pancake £6.25, chicken fillets in garlic sauce £7.25, fillet of lamb with cherry and almond sauce £7.50 and medallions of fillet steak with horseradish and walnut sauce £10.50.

The White Hart is open 11.00 - 15.00 and 18.00 - 23.00 with normal Sunday hours. There is a patio area, a large beer garden and children's area with wild cats, sheep, chicken and rabbits.

Seasonal activities, skittle alley and function room for hire. Dogs are allowed, there are five large pub dogs! Access and Visa welcome.

Ringwood Road, Netley Marsh, near Cadnam. Tel (01703) 862166

The White Horse has recently undergone major refurbishment but remains a comfortable village inn on the edge on the New Forest, hosted by John and Denise Randall.

Real ales include Flowers Original, Boddingtons, Wadworth 6X, Old Speckled Hen and Gales HSB. Whitbread Best, Murphys stout, Heineken, Stella Artois and Stongbow cider are also on draught.

Food is good value for money and includes man-sized sandwiches from £1.40, prawn cocktail £2.30, jumbo cod fillet in batter £4.25, cottage pie £4, venison pie £4.50, chilli con carne £4.25, gammon steak £4.75 and 8oz. sirloin steak £8.25. Traditional Sunday lunch served.

The White House is open 11.00 - 15.00 and 17.30 - 23.00 six days a week with normal Sunday hours. Popular live entertainment every Tuesday evening.

THE WHITE ROSE HOTEL   128

Village Centre, Sway. Tel (01590) 682754

Right in the centre of Sway this Edwardian country house offers a relaxed hotel bar with bamboo furniture, piano and garden views. Occasional live entertainment makes this the focal point of the village.

Ringwood Best and Ringwood Fortyniner are served at pub prices on hand-pump. Bass Special Bitter, Worthington Best Bitter, Guinness, Carling Black Label, Tennent's Extra and Dry Blackthorn cider are also on draught.

Food prices are slightly above average for a pub but specials include seafood salad £5.50 and grilled salmon £7. Reasonable table d'hote and extensive á la carte offered in the restaurant.

The bar is open 11.00 - 23.00 six days a week. Normal Sunday hours except for privileged hotel guests.

Accommodation from £39 single and £29 per person double. Dogs by arrangement.

WINE PRESS   129

Montagu Arms Hotel, Palace Lane, Beaulieu. Tel (01590) 612324

This popular drinking establishment is full of charm as it is located adjacent to one of the best hotels in the area and close to Lord Montagu's National Motor Museum and at the start of a most picturesque and enjoyable walk to Bucklers Hard. It is difficult to decide whether the Wine Press is more a pub or a wine bar, certainly the clientele treat it as their local, but the dark green decor, vine leaves and trellis give it a wine bar appearance. The bar is nevertheless comfortably furnished and has an open fire.

The first recorded vineyard at Beaulieu was set up in 1735 by John 2nd Duke of Montagu, but the vineyard proved to be unprofitable and was closed ten years later. However, it was re-established thirty years ago and produces a medium dry white wine which is available by the bottle £12.95 on the extensive wine list.

Real ale choices include Flowers Original, Wadworth 6X and Boddingtons Bitter. Whitbread Best, Guinness, Heineken, Heineken Export, Stella Artois, Strongbow and Scrumpy Jack cider are also available on draught and there is an extensive range of bottled beers to choose from.

There is both a snack menu and a list featuring more substantial, traditional dishes. At lunchtime the blackboard menu may highlight spicy bean casserole served with homemade bread £3.95, Hampshire ham salad £4.95 and beef and mushrooms in a rich wine sauce £4.95. In the evening dining is more formal with the blackboard listing dishes like fingers of venison served in a Madeira sauce £7.50, confit of duck served in an orange sauce £7.95 and spicy vegetarian casserole served with tagliatelli £3.95.

The Wine Press is open all day except on Sundays when the usual hours apply. Children, but not dogs are welcome inside, and all credit cards are accepted. Entertainment ranges from background music, pool and darts, to monthly live music during the winter. Well appointed accommodation next door from £70 per night.

Sopley, near Bransgore. Tel (01425) 672252   * "Don't Miss" award

We are not saying that you should not miss this pub simply because the landlord presented my mother with a birthday bottle of champagne, but because of the friendly staff, the good food, the unique location and the excellent management. The Woolpack is a charming, olde-worlde, 17th century, thatched coaching inn in which landlords Dick and Barbara Goemaatt have successfully created a cosy and welcoming atmosphere. It is a very popular venue, especially in summer. Inside, several comfortable beamed seating areas radiate out from the single bar and there are two open fires, a conservatory restaurant and Wendy house for children, all, thankfully, juke box and electronic game free. A delightful terrace garden overlooks a pretty stream, complete with a complement of ducks and a bridge to the children's play area.

This is a Whitbread property dispensing their Best Bitter, Murphys stout, Guinness, Heineken, Heineken Export, Stella Artois, Red Rock and Dry Blackthorn cider on draught, plus real ales - Ringwood Best Bitter, Wadworth 6X and Flowers Original - on handpump.

The menu is innovative, the food excellent and particularly pleasing is that all the dishes are reasonably priced at around £5 - £7. Choices include cod in beer batter £5.50, avocado bake topped with red peppers and cheese £4.95, deep-fried breaded seafood platter £5.50, fresh salmon steak poached in white wine and herbs £6.95, cod and prawn au gratin £5.95, crispy gammon hock in honey and cider sauce £5.25 and lamb noisettes in Dijonnaise sauce £5.95. Try also the Dutch open rolls, beef or lightly smoked ham £2.95.

The Woolpack is open 11.00 - 23.00 except Sunday when the normal hours apply. Credit cards are accepted. Dogs are welcome in the bar, as are children in the family room only. Pianist plays every night.